Francis Frith's
VICTORIAN & EDWARDIAN
MARITIME ALBUM

◆

Francis Frith's

VICTORIAN & EDWARDIAN MARITIME ALBUM

◆

Clive Hardy

First published in the United Kingdom in 2000 by
Frith Book Company Ltd

Hardback Edition 2000
ISBN 1-85937-144-2

Paperback Edition 2002
ISBN 1-85937-622-3

British Library Cataloguing in Publication Data

Francis Frith's Victorian & Edwardian Maritime Album
Clive Hardy

Frith Book Company Ltd
Frith's Barn, Teffont,
Salisbury, Wiltshire SP3 5QP
Tel: +44 (0) 1722 716 376
Email: info@francisfrith.co.uk
www.francisfrith.co.uk

Printed and bound in Great Britain

AS WITH ANY HISTORICAL DATABASE THE FRITH ARCHIVE IS CONSTANTLY BEING CORRECTED AND IMPROVED
AND THE PUBLISHERS WOULD WELCOME INFORMATION ON OMISSIONS OR INACCURACIES

Contents

Francis Frith: Victorian Pioneer   7

Frith's Archive - A Unique Legacy   10

Victorian & Edwardian Maritime Album
An Introduction   12

The Royal Navy   18

Channel Packets, Excursion Steamers
& Ferries   30

Around the Ports and Harbours   52

Working Boats   120

Index   131

Free Mounted Print Voucher   *135*

FRANCIS FRITH: *Victorian Pioneer*

FRANCIS FRITH, Victorian founder of the world-famous photographic archive, was a complex and fascinating man. A devout Quaker and a highly successful Victorian businessman, he was both philosophic by nature and pioneering in outlook.

By 1855 Francis Frith had already established a wholesale grocery business in Liverpool, and sold it for the astonishing sum of £200,000, which is the equivalent today of over £15,000,000. Now a multi-millionaire, he was able to indulge his passion for travel. As a child he had pored over travel books written by early explorers, and his fancy and imagination had been stirred by family holidays to the sublime mountain regions of Wales and Scotland. 'What a land of spirit-stirring and enriching scenes and places!' he had written. He was to return to these scenes of grandeur in later years to 'recapture the thousands of vivid and tender memories', but with a different purpose. Now in his thirties, and captivated by the new science of photography, Frith set out on a series of pioneering journeys to the Nile regions that occupied him from 1856 until 1860.

INTRIGUE AND ADVENTURE

He took with him on his travels a specially-designed wicker carriage that acted as both dark-room and sleeping chamber. These far-flung journeys were packed with intrigue and adventure. In his life story, written when he was sixty-three, Frith tells of being held captive by bandits, and of fighting 'an awful midnight battle to the very point of surrender with a deadly pack of hungry, wild dogs'. Sporting flowing Arab costume, Frith arrived at Akaba by camel seventy years before Lawrence, where he encountered 'desert princes and rival sheikhs, blazing with jewel-hilted swords'.

During these extraordinary adventures he was assiduously exploring the desert regions bordering the Nile and patiently recording the antiquities and peoples with his camera. He was the first photographer to venture beyond the sixth cataract. Africa was still the mysterious 'Dark Continent', and Stanley and Livingstone's historic meeting was a decade into the future. The conditions for picture taking confound belief. He laboured for hours in his wicker dark-room in the sweltering heat of the desert, while the volatile chemicals fizzed dangerously in their trays. Often he was forced to work in remote tombs and caves where conditions were cooler. Back in London he exhibited his photographs and was 'rapturously cheered' by members of the Royal Society. His reputation as a photographer was made overnight. An eminent modern historian has likened their impact on the population of the time to that on our own generation of the first photographs taken on the surface of the moon.

VENTURE OF A LIFE-TIME

Characteristically, Frith quickly spotted the opportunity to create a new business as a specialist publisher of photographs. He lived in an era of immense and sometimes violent change. For the poor in the early part of Victoria's reign work was a drudge and the hours long, and people had precious little free time to enjoy themselves.

Most had no transport other than a cart or gig at their disposal, and had not travelled far beyond the boundaries of their own town or village. However, by the 1870s, the railways had threaded their way across the country, and Bank Holidays and half-day Saturdays had been made obligatory by Act of Parliament. All of a sudden the ordinary working man and his family were able to enjoy days out and see a little more of the world.

With characteristic business acumen, Francis Frith foresaw that these new tourists would enjoy having souvenirs to commemorate their days out. In 1860 he married Mary Ann Rosling and set out with the intention of photographing every city, town and village in Britain. For the next thirty years he travelled the country by train and by pony and trap, producing fine photographs of seaside resorts and beauty spots that were keenly bought by millions of Victorians. These prints were painstakingly pasted into family albums and pored over during the dark nights of winter, rekindling precious memories of summer excursions.

THE RISE OF FRITH & CO

Frith's studio was soon supplying retail shops all over the country. To meet the demand he gathered about him a small team of photographers, and published the work of independent artist-photographers of the calibre of Roger Fenton and Francis Bedford. In order to gain some understanding of the scale of Frith's business one only has to look at the catalogue issued by Frith & Co in 1886: it

runs to some 670 pages, listing not only many thousands of views of the British Isles but also many photographs of most European countries, and China, Japan, the USA and Canada – note the sample page shown above from the hand-written *Frith & Co* ledgers detailing pictures taken. By 1890 Frith had created the greatest specialist photographic publishing company in the world, with over 2,000 outlets – more than the combined number that Boots and WH Smith have today! The picture on the right shows the *Frith & Co* display board at Ingleton in the Yorkshire Dales. Beautifully constructed with mahogany frame and gilt inserts, it could display up to a dozen local scenes.

POSTCARD BONANZA

The ever-popular holiday postcard we know today took many years to develop. In 1870 the Post Office issued the first plain cards, with a pre-printed stamp on one face. In 1894 they allowed other publishers' cards to be sent through the mail with an attached adhesive halfpenny stamp. Demand grew rapidly, and in 1895 a new size of postcard

was permitted called the court card, but there was little room for illustration. In 1899, a year after Frith's death, a new card measuring 5.5 x 3.5 inches became the standard format, but it was not until 1902 that the divided back came into being, with address and message on one face and a full-size illustration on the other. *Frith & Co* were in the vanguard of postcard development, and Frith's sons Eustace and Cyril continued their father's monumental task, expanding the number of views offered to the public and recording more and more places in Britain, as the coasts and countryside were opened up to mass travel.

Francis Frith died in 1898 at his villa in Cannes, his great project still growing. The archive he created continued in business for another seventy years. By 1970 it contained over a third of a million pictures of 7,000 cities, towns and villages. The massive photographic record Frith has left to us stands as a living monument to a special and very remarkable man.

Frith's Archive: *A Unique Legacy*

FRANCIS FRITH'S legacy to us today is of immense significance and value, for the magnificent archive of evocative photographs he created provides a unique record of change in 7,000 cities, towns and villages throughout Britain over a century and more. Frith and his fellow studio photographers revisited locations many times down the years to update their views, compiling for us an enthralling and colourful pageant of British life and character.

We tend to think of Frith's sepia views of Britain as nostalgic, for most of us use them to conjure up memories of places in our own lives with which we have family associations. It often makes us forget that to Francis Frith they were records of daily life as it was actually being lived in the cities, towns and villages of his day. The Victorian age was one of great and often bewildering change for ordinary people, and though the pictures evoke an impression of slower times, life was as busy and hectic as it is today.

We are fortunate that Frith was a photographer of the people, dedicated to recording the minutiae of everyday life. For it is this sheer wealth of visual data, the painstaking chronicle of changes in dress, transport, street layouts, buildings, housing, engineering and landscape that captivates us so much today. His remarkable images offer us a powerful link with the past and with the lives of our ancestors.

TODAY'S TECHNOLOGY

Computers have now made it possible for Frith's many thousands of images to be accessed almost instantly. In the Frith archive today, each photograph is carefully 'digitised' then stored on a CD Rom. Frith archivists can locate a single photograph amongst thousands within seconds. Views can be catalogued and sorted under a variety of categories of place and content to the immediate benefit of researchers. Inexpensive reference prints can be created for them at the touch of a mouse button, and a wide range of books and other printed materials assembled and published for a wider, more general readership - in the next twelve months over a hundred Frith local history titles will be published! The day-to-

See Frith at www.francisfrith.co.uk

day workings of the archive are very different from how they were in Francis Frith's time: imagine the herculean task of sorting through eleven tons of glass negatives as Frith had to do to locate a particular sequence of pictures! Yet the archive still prides itself on maintaining the same high standards of excellence laid down by Francis Frith, including the painstaking cataloguing and indexing of every view.

It is curious to reflect on how the internet now allows researchers in America and elsewhere greater instant access to the archive than Frith himself ever enjoyed. Many thousands of individual views can be called up on screen within seconds on one of the Frith internet sites, enabling people living continents away to revisit the streets of their ancestral home town, or view places in Britain where they have enjoyed holidays. Many overseas researchers welcome the chance to view special theme selections, such as transport, sports, costume and ancient monuments.

We are certain that Francis Frith would have heartily approved of these modern developments, for he himself was always working at the very limits of Victorian photographic technology.

THE VALUE OF THE ARCHIVE TODAY

Because of the benefits brought by the computer, Frith's images are increasingly studied by social historians, by researchers into genealogy and ancestory, by architects, town planners, and by teachers and schoolchildren involved in local history projects. In addition, the archive offers every one of us a unique opportunity to examine the places where we and our families have lived and worked down the years. Immensely successful in Frith's own era, the archive is now, a century and more on, entering a new phase of popularity.

THE PAST IN TUNE WITH THE FUTURE

Historians consider the Francis Frith Collection to be of prime national importance. It is the only archive of its kind remaining in private ownership and has been valued at a million pounds. However, this figure is now rapidly increasing as digital technology enables more and more people around the world to enjoy its benefits.

Francis Frith's archive is now housed in an historic timber barn in the beautiful village of Teffont in Wiltshire. Its founder would not recognize the archive office as it is today. In place of the many thousands of dusty boxes containing glass plate negatives and an all-pervading odour of photographic chemicals, there are now ranks of computer screens. He would be amazed to watch his images travelling round the world at unimaginable speeds through network and internet lines.

The archive's future is both bright and exciting. Francis Frith, with his unshakeable belief in making photographs available to the greatest number of people, would undoubtedly approve of what is being done today with his lifetime's work. His photographs, depicting our shared past, are now bringing pleasure and enlightenment to millions around the world a century and more after his death.

VICTORIAN & EDWARDIAN MARITIME ALBUM
An Introduction

THE TRANSFORMATION IN shipping that took place during the Victorian and Edwardian eras did not happen in splendid isolation, but as a direct result of economic, political and social influences both at home and abroad. The first section of the book looks at the Royal Navy, then the most powerful in the world, even if was not always in the vanguard when it came to change and technical innovation. When Queen Victoria visited Napoleon III on board the French warship 'Bretagne' at Cherbourg in 1858, ship design had hardly changed from the time of the Napoleonic Wars. True, there were steam-powered fighting ships in both fleets, but apart from a handful of vessels such as France's 'Napoleon' (1850) and the Royal Navy's 'Agamemnon' (1852), the steam engine was used for auxiliary power only, whilst guns continued to be mounted broadside. In 1845 Brunel had pointed the way for future ship development when he staged his now famous trial of strength

between the experimental screw steamer 'Rattler' and the paddler 'Alecto'. The ships, joined stern to stern by strong cables, were to steam ahead in a nautical tug o' war: 'Rattler's' propeller eventually got the better of 'Alecto's' paddles and pulled her backwards through the water. The experiment confirmed that the screw was a better proposition than the paddle-wheel and influenced both naval and merchant ship design.

In 1859 the French took the lead again when they commissioned the 'La Gloire', the world's first armoured warship, with iron plates nailed over her wooden hull. The Royal Navy responded by building the iron-plated frigate 'Warrior'. A naval arms race seemed to be on the cards, but events the other side of the Atlantic did not go unnoticed by Europe's naval powers. The American Civil War was the first modern war, using trenches, barbed wire, rapid-fire guns, and railways to transport troops and supplies. The wars at sea saw the

Confederates use commerce raiders and fast blockade runners. Most famous of all, though, was their 'Merrimac', a former frigate which had been rebuilt from the waterline upwards. Sheathed in iron so thick that Union cannon balls bounced off her sloping sides, she steamed slowly into action against Federal warships in Hampton Roads. But the North knew all about her and had not been idle. They had commissioned the engineer John Ericsson to come up with a suitable response; this he did in the shape of the 'Monitor', a steam-powered armoured warship with an exceptionally low freeboard, mounting one of the first armoured gun turrets. The clash between 'Monitor' and 'Merrimac' was indecisive, but the monitor as a type of warship was taken up world wide; the Royal Navy found a use for them in both world wars.

By the end of Victoria's reign, the torpedo, submarine and airship had all made their appearance. The torpedo was only taken seriously after a Chilean ironclad was sunk by such a weapon during the Nitrate Wars. Richard Whitehead had perfected an effective torpedo by 1866, but the Admiralty declined to offer him the facilities he needed, and he finished up going to Fiume in Italy, where he was made welcome. The torpedo threat caused navies to equip their ships with quick-firing guns and anti-torpedo nets for additional protection when at anchor.

By 1900 Britain no longer regarded France as a threat. There was a new possible danger, a unified Germany. The German High Seas Fleet was seen as a direct challenge to the Royal Navy; though Britain gained the edge in 1906 with the completion of the 21-knot turbine-driven super battleship HMS 'Dreadnought', it was short-lived. With all earlier battleships effectively obsolete, Britain was leading Germany by just one ship, and a naval arms race was the only outcome. The ships were designed for different roles. Those of the High Seas Fleet were to operate in the North Sea and the Baltic, never far from their bases. German designers could sacrifice fuel and crew comfort (when in home port the crews slept in barracks ashore) for armour and superb watertight integrity of the hulls. The battleships of the Royal Navy had to be able to go anywhere in the world, to operate in any climate, and carry fuel, stores and spares. Armour had to be sacrificed for greater operational ranges. By the end of the Edwardian era the Royal Navy's livery of black hulls, white upperworks, yellow ochre masts, vents and funnels, had given way to battleship grey.

The most important naval conflict that happened during the period occurred on the other side of the world. During the Russo-Japanese War of 1904-05, the world's press reported the fortunes of Russia's Baltic Fleet as it slowly made its way half way round the globe, only to be destroyed by Admiral Heihachiro Togo in the Tsushima Straits. Russia had already been humiliated by the Japanese both on land and at sea, and the despatch of her Baltic Fleet was a last desperate attempt to redress the balance. The fleet had at its core a few modern battleships and cruisers, but beyond that it was a rag-tag outfit of obsolete rust-buckets that should have been confined to harbour duties. Matters were made worse by the fact that too few of its officers had attained their ranks through their abilities as professional seaman; many were aristocrats who held rank by patronage. Many of the ordinary sailors were conscripted peasants who had never even seen the sea before, let alone sailed upon it.

On the other hand, after centuries of imposed isolation Japan had enthusiastically embraced the industrialisation process from the 1870s onwards, adopting Western technology, institutions, and even fashions. Though Japanese society hung on to many of its feudal traditions, it was a modern Japanese

army that had defeated the Chinese in 1894, and it was a well-equipped Japanese force that had taken part in the international relief force sent to Peking during the Boxer Rebellion in 1900. Japan's army was trained by the best: the Prussians. Her navy was built in Britain, and its officers were sent to learn their trade at Greenwich.

Within days of leaving the Baltic, the Russians caused an international incident and brought Europe to the brink of war: they shelled British fishing vessels in the North Sea in the belief that they were Japanese torpedo boats. They also managed to fire on one another. The Russians were escorted to the Mediterranean by British battleships as the press screamed for revenge, demanding that the officers responsible be brought back to England, by force if necessary, to stand trial for the murder of British fishermen.

At the beginning of the 20th century, gunnery practice for ships of the Royal Navy was at ranges of between 2000 and 3000 yards against static targets; the Imperial German Navy, on the other hand, had opened the range to around 5000 yards against towed targets. The foreign observers aboard Admiral Togo's ships were in for a shock when the Japanese opened fire at an unprecedented 14,000 yards. Japanese

professionalism and accurate gunfire soon told, and the Baltic Fleet ceased to exist. This resounding victory reinforced Japan's status as the leading military power in the Far East; it also caused the lights to burn late into the night in the Admiralties and Foreign Offices of the colonial powers.

In the remaining chapters we look at cross-channel packets, excursion steamers, inshore craft, ports and harbours. The excursion steamer market remained a last stronghold for paddle-steamers long after they had been replaced on deep sea routes; they survived well into the 20th century. We also visit a number of ports and harbours, ranging from the tiny fishing village of Polperro and the china clay ports of Fowey and Charlestown, to Liverpool, Bristol, Barry and Manchester. Opened by Queen Victoria in 1894, the Manchester Ship Canal was completed at a cost of £14.3 million, and was one of the great civil engineering masterpieces of the age. Construction of the 36-mile-long waterway involved the excavation and removal of 48 million cubic yards of earth, and the building of locks to lift the canal to sixty feet above sea level at Manchester. The locks allowed for ships with maximum dimensions of 600ft x 65ft x 28ft draught x 70ft headroom to navigate its entire length. Traffic for the first

year of operation amounted to 299,407 tons of exports and 386,751 tons of imports. In 1897 total imports broke through the one million tons barrier, with exports at a healthy 616,812 tons. Ten years later imports were 2,500,000 tons, and exports 2,300,000 tons. Before the canal opened, Manchester as a port was ranked 116th in Great Britain; by the end of 1906 it was 4th. There had been a proposal to construct the canal at sea level along its entire length, like the lock-free Suez Canal. Had this been done, the Port of Manchester would have then been located in a big hole in the ground, resulting in problems for rail and road access.

Among the Liverpool pictures is one of the White Star Liner 'Adriatic', built in 1872, and the first ship to be fitted with gas lighting, even if it was restricted to the passenger accommodation only. The gas was generated by heating oil; the vapour was then circulated to between 30 and 40 burners, each of twelve candle power. Though initially a success, the equipment was removed because the rigid pipework was constantly being ruptured by the motion and vibration of the ship. Nine years later, Cunard's 'Servia' would be the first liner to have a comprehensive electric lighting system, including in the engine and boiler rooms.

On the transatlantic route, improvements in ship design and comfort came thick and fast as the shipping lines tried to outdo one another in order to secure the patronage of wealthy Americans wishing to visit Europe. The improvements were not all British-led. The American Collins Line was the first to equip a ship with an ice room so that its passengers could dine on otherwise unobtainable dishes, and it was the first to provide passengers with proper bathrooms. For almost thirty years the paddle-liner had dominated the Atlantic, but in 1866 Tod & McGregor of Glasgow completed the iron-hulled screw steamer 'City of Paris' for the Inman Line of Liverpool. Fitted with a two-cylinder horizontal trunk engine, the 2651 grt liner could make 13 knots. The iron hull had already proved its worth on the New York run. On 23 January 1856 the Collins Line 'Pacific', a wooden-hulled paddler, had steamed out of Liverpool with 45 passengers and 141 crew on board. The following day Cunard's new iron-hulled paddler 'Persia' left Liverpool, the intention being that she should not only catch the 'Pacific' but overhaul her and beat her into New York. Five days into the voyage, 'Persia' ran into an ice field, sustaining damage to her bow, starboard side and starboard paddle-box. Though she was down

by the head, Captain Judkins succeeded in bringing her into New York. Of the 'Pacific' there was no sign; in fact, she was never heard of again. It is assumed that she had run into the same ice field at speed and had been sunk.

But it would be during the Edwardian era that one of the greatest sea mysteries of modern times took place. In October 1908 Blue Anchor Line had taken delivery of their new 9339 grt liner 'Waratah' from Barclay, Curle. She was a twin-screw ship with quadruple-expansion engines, and was fitted out for the emigrant trade to Australia. 'Waratah' left Adelaide on her homeward run on 7 July 1909, arriving at Durban to coal and take on passengers on the 25th. She sailed the following day for Cape Town, and was seen in the early hours of the 27th by the steamer 'Clan MacIntyre'. 'Waratah' sailed over the horizon and was never seen again. What made her disappearance all the more mysterious is that despite an intensive search and rescue operation nothing was ever found, not even a lifebelt. If she had stayed upon her presumed course, she would have run into a severe gale on the 29th, which at the time was described as the worst in living memory. It is assumed that she foundered. One of the alternative theories was that her engines had failed and

that she had drifted towards Antarctica on the Agulhas current. A ship was sent south to look for her amid the ice, but again nothing was ever found.

One of the pictures of Barry Docks features a line of full-rigged merchant sailing ships loading with coal. In 1864 Liverpool merchant Samuel Rathbone had said that 'steamships may occupy the Mediterranean, may tentatively go to Brazil and the Plate - but China at least is safe for sailing ships'. In November 1869 Empress Eugenie of France opened the Suez Canal. The new route cut 3300 miles off the journey from Britain to China, making it an economical proposition for steamship owners once bunkering ports had been established. Only the previous year, Aberdeen Line had taken delivery of the 991 grt clipper 'Thermopylae'. Composite-hulled, ship-rigged and with a distinctive jib-boom, she turned out to be a ship of outstanding qualities. On her maiden voyage to Melbourne under the command of Captain Kemball, she set what has become an unbeaten record for sail of sixty days from the Lizard. She then set the record for the run from Newcastle, New South Wales to Shanghai, taking just 28 days instead of the more usual six to eight weeks. Only one ship ever came close to catching her, and that was the 'Cutty Sark'. The opening of the Suez Canal and the increasing reliability of marine engines would see the clippers relegated to the Australian wool trade, where capacity and not speed was important. But sail was not quite finished. During the late 1880s and early 1890s, it experienced something of a renaissance, thanks to steel becoming readily available owing to mills becoming equipped with Bessemer converters. This enabled large steel-hulled merchant sailing ships equipped with labour-saving devices to be built, and for a few years they were able to compete against steamships in the bulk cargo market, carrying coal, timber, nitrate and grain.

By 1900 Britain's merchant fleet (not including Dominion and colonial tonnage) carried over 50 per cent of world trade in 11.5 million tons of steam and 1.7 million tons of sailing ships. Our nearest rivals were France with just 1.1 million tons, and Germany with 2.2 million tons of steamships. By 1910 the British merchant fleet stood at 16.8 million tons of steam and 750,000 tons of sailing ships. British owners continued to use sail in the coastal trade and the fishing industry, but here too, as the technological advances cascaded down to smaller ships, steam was making inroads.

The Royal Navy

DEVONPORT

HMS Magnificent 1898 41938

A unit of the Majestic class of nine battleships completed between 1895 and 1898 at a cost of approximately £1 million each. Displacing 14,000 tons, 'Magnificent' and two of her sisters, 'Victorious' and 'Illustrious', were built at Chatham. The main battery comprised 4 x 12-inch mark VIII, 35 calibre guns with an arc of fire of 260 degrees; the secondary battery consisted of 12 x 6-inch. Close-in defence was provided for in the shape of 16 x 12-pdrs, 12 x 3-pdrs, 2 Maxims and 5 x 18-inch torpedo tubes, and a midships net defence against torpedo attack when at anchor. The total weight of ammunition carried was 355 tons. The Majestics carried over 4000 tons of armour plate, varying in thickness from 4 inches on the deck slopes to 14 inches on the conning tower and barbettes. The hull was divided into 150 watertight compartments with a total of 208 watertight doors. These ships had two funnels; placed side-by-side instead of the more traditional fore and aft.

LIVERPOOL
HMS Belleisle 1890 24421

HMS 'Belleisle' was a coast defence central battery armoured ship.
Resplendent in her Victorian livery of black hull, white
upperworks, yellow ochre masts and funnel, she was built at Poplar
in 1878, engined by Maudsley and purchased by the Admiralty for
£240,000. She displaced 4870 tons, and her length overall was
245ft, beam 52ft and draught 21ft. In 1890 she could manage 12.2
knots, though she was much happier doing ten; but by 1895 her
speed seems to have been reduced to an asthmatic 8.4 knots. Her
armament comprised 4 x 25-ton MLRs; 6 x 6-pdr QFs, nine
machine guns and a launch carriage for torpedoes.

◆

LIVERPOOL, HMS HERCULES 1890 24422

HMS 'Hercules' was a centre battery ironclad battleship. Designed in 1865 and built at Chatham, she was completed in 1868 at a cost of £361,134 including machinery. 'Hercules' was 325ft in length with a beam of 59ft and a draught of 26.5ft, and she displaced 8680 tons. She was a regular visitor to the Mersey, along with other units of the channel fleet. A problem with warships like 'Hercules' was that though they carried an impressive range of weaponry, they lacked firepower at the bow and stern.

KINGSTOWN, HMS PELORUS 1897 39311

Laid down at Sheerness in 1895, engined by Clydebank, and completed in 1897, 'Pelorus' was the lead ship for a class of seven cruisers. After serving with the Channel Fleet, 'Pelorus' spent the years 1904-1909 on the Cape Station before transferring to the East Indies. During the Great War she was deployed in the Mediterranean, and was sold for breaking up in 1920.

KINGSTOWN, PELORUS CLASS CRUISER 1897 39312

The seven ships of the Pelorus class were completed between 1897 and 1900. When built they were rated as first-class cruisers; however, they were under-gunned, mounting only 8 x 4-inch, 8 x 3-pdrs and 2 x 14-inch torpedo tubes, and their deck armour was only two inches thick. From the numbering system used by the Frith archive, it appears that this picture was taken on the same visit to Kingstown as photograph No 31311. If that is correct, then this ship is either the 'Pegasus' or the 'Prosperine', as the other four vessels in the class were still building.

KINGSTOWN, THE HARBOUR 1897 39310

This is a 3400 tons displacement Apollo class cruiser. Completed in the early 1890s, the Apollos, of which there were 21, were rated as second-class protected cruisers and armed with 2 x 6-inch, 6 x 4.7-inch, 8 x 6-pdrs, 1 x 3-pdr and 4 x 14-inch torpedo tubes. Funnel details indicate that this ship may be either the 'Melampus', the 'Naiad' or the 'Latona'. By 1914 only the 'Sappho', the 'Sirius' and the 'Melpomene' (ex 'Indefatigable') were still rated as cruisers; the others had been converted into minelayers.

GRAVESEND
HMS Gleaner 1902 49043

By the early 1890s, the Fiume Whitehead 18-inch torpedo had a range varying from 440 yds to about 900 yds. Close-range torpedoes could carry a warhead of about 220 lbs of gun cotton and travel at about 32 knots; long-range torpedoes carried a lighter warhead and at travelled at a slightly slower speed. When the Chilean ironclad 'Blanco Encalada' was attacked and sunk by two small boats armed with primitive torpedoes, the world's navies began at last to take the torpedo seriously. The idea that small and relatively inexpensive, highly manoeuvrable, fast attack craft had the potential to wreak havoc amid a squadron of very big, very slow and very expensive ironclads, called for counter measures. One was the close-range quick-firing gun; the other was the first-class torpedo gunboat. HMS 'Gleaner' cost £63,798, and was completed at Sheerness in 1890. Displacing 735 tons, she was armed with 1 x 4.7-inch QF and 4 x 3-pdr QFs. Her speed of 20.1 knots meant that she could intercept most torpedo boats in service in 1890, though by 1892 the French were already planning 30 knot attack craft.

DEVONPORT
HMS Impregnable 1893 31959

Until the 1850s, the Navy offered little in the way of pre-sea training to recruits; they were simply posted to a ship, where they learned their craft from experienced hands. In 1854 the ageing 74-gun warship HMS 'Illustrious' was given a new lease of life when she was commissioned as a harbour training ship for young seamen. In 1857 her role was extended when she received her first batch of officer cadets. It was soon apparent that 'Illustrious' was too small for all that was required of her, and in January 1859 HMS 'Britannia' (120 guns) was commissioned under Capt Robert Harris to act as a training ship for would-be officers. She was joined in 1864 by HMS 'Hindostan', which was moored ahead of her. Five years later 'Britannia' was relieved and replaced by the 1861-built steam warship 'Prince of Wales', which was then renamed 'Britannia'. In 1905 the Royal Naval College, Dartmouth was opened, and both 'Britannia' and 'Hindostan' were paid off.

DEVENPORT, HMS IMPREGNABLE 1904 52416

A large number of wooden walls were retained by the Navy for various harbour duties. Some served as training ships, others were reduced to storage and coal hulks. Among the wooden walls to be seen at Devonport around 1904 were the gunnery training ships 'Cambridge' and 'Calcutta', the torpedo schoolship 'Defiance', the receiving ship 'Circe', and the training ships 'Lion' and 'Implacable'.

DEVONPORT, HMS ROYAL ADELAIDE 1890 22465

This is a fine view of the 'Royal Adelaide' (104 guns). Laid down at Plymouth Dockyard as HMS 'London' in 1819, her name was changed during her somewhat slow construction; she was not launched until July 1828. 'Royal Adelaide' was one of the first ships of the line to have planking right round the bow at the height of the forecastle. The weakest part of all wooden warships from the age of sail was the stern. There are numerous accounts of the destruction caused and carnage wreaked by a warship crossing the stern of another and raking it with gunfire at close quarters. The original specification for 'Royal Adelaide' called for the strengthening of the stern and reducing the size of the windows in the officers' quarters. Officers raised such objections that the plans were dropped and her stern remained open.

PLYMOUTH 1892 30585
Two brigs belonging to the Training Squadron ease their way pass
Drake's Island. It was in the Training Squadron that the majority of
recruits got their first taste of life at sea, though for them it appears
to have been little different to what it had been like in Nelson's day,
with similar rations and strict discipline; even the gunnery drills
were carried out with muzzle-loading cannon, handspikes and
tackles having to be used to traverse the guns. Boys who joined aged
about 17 were sent aboard the 'Calliope' or the 'Northampton'.
The brigs included the 'Pilot', the 'Nautilus' (tender to HMS
'Lion'), the 'Liberty' (tender to HMS 'Implacable'), and the
'Martin' (floating classroom for HMS 'Impregnable').

PORTSMOUTH HARBOUR 1898
42703

HMS' St Vincent' (120 guns) was completed in 1815, but too late to take an active part in the Napoleonic Wars. In fact, she was not commissioned until 1831, when she was sent to the Mediterranean as Flagship. There followed spells as Flagship, Portsmouth; Guardship in Ordinary at Portsmouth; and as a naval transport during the Crimean War. In 1862 she became a boys' training ship, a role she fulfilled until 1906 when she was sent for breaking up.

PORTSMOUTH HARBOUR 1898 42704
In the centre of the picture are a
number of coal and stores hulks,
and also what appears to be the
turret-ship HMS 'Conqueror', built
at Chatham and carrying a main
armament of 2 x 45-ton guns. Over
on the right is one of the new breed
of four-funnelled cruisers them
coming into service, while the small
twin-funnelled vessel on the left of
the picture might be the survey ship
HMS 'Hearty' (1885), though it
could also be the special service
vessel HMS 'Magnet' (1883).

PORTSMOUTH HARBOUR 1898

42705

Here we see one of the unsung heroes of the Fleet. Major naval bases such as Portsmouth, Plymouth and Malta found employment for a host of small craft - tenders, tugs, lighters, and ferries - not all of them necessarily owned by the Royal Navy. Here the 'Frances' scurries past our photographer.

DOVER, ADMIRALTY PIER 1901

48058A

Dover was designated a naval base and coaling station. By 1914 the harbour covered 610 acres, parts of which were still 30ft deep at low water. Moorings were provided for 16 battleships, 5 large cruisers and 11 smaller cruisers as well as destroyers. There was also a submarine base here.

Channel Packets, Excursion Steamers & Ferries

ROTHESAY, THE PIER 1897 39836

As one paddler loads, another leaves. It is 1897, and a golden age for the Clyde excursion steamer industry is dawning: operators sense that the ban on landings at some piers on the Sabbath will soon be broken. The paddler pulling away might be the 'Ivanhoe', shortly after her sale to the Caledonian Steam Packet Co, but before her paddle-boxes were painted white and a bar installed. At 282 grt, 'Ivanhoe' had been built in 1880 by D & W Henderson for the Firth of Clyde Steam Packet Co as a temperance ship. Everyone said that the idea would never work, but it did; she proved very popular with families desperate to avoid having to mix with the heavy drinkers, who often made trips miserable for everyone except for themselves. The ship was always immaculately turned out, and her crew wore naval uniform. In 1894 she spent a couple of months on charter on excursion work along the newly opened Manchester Ship Canal, but returned north in time for the summer season.

DUNOON
PS Columba 1904 52621
Launched on 11 April 1878, the Clyde paddler 'Columba' was the
last vessel built for David Hutchinson & Co; the firm changed its
name to David Macbrayne the following year. Ordered for the
Glasgow-Tarbert-Ardrishaig run, 'Columba' was not only the first
Clyde paddler fitted with full-width passenger saloons, but she also
had a bookshop, hairdressing saloon, fruit stall and post office. Her
design speed of 18 knots at 36rpm was improved upon in 1900
when she was fitted with haystack boilers, making her capable of 19
knots at 40 rpm. In September 1936 she was laid up at Greenock
for the last time and sold the following March for scrap. She was
broken up at Dalmuir.

ABERDOUR
The Pier 1897 39147

Excursion trips flourished on the east coast of Scotland until 2 August 1914, when the Admiralty effectively closed the Firth of Forth to non-essential shipping. Well-patronised excursions had included Leith to the Fife resorts and then up to Dundee, and Leith to Alloa and Stirling. Those short of funds could take a non-landing trip to Burntisland for 10d return. One of the companies active on the Forth was the Galloway Saloon Steam Packet Co. Founded in June 1886, it was acquired a few years later by the North British Steam Packet Co, a subsidiary of the North British Railway. However, the GSSPCo retained its old title, and was left very much to its own devices. Between 1886 and 1900 the Forth was livened up when the GSSPCo broke away from the more sombre liveries of the day: it gave its paddlers lavender-coloured hulls with a red waterline, white paddle-box facings, yellow funnels and varnished woodwork.

GREENOCK, PRINCES PIER 1904 52634
In 1869 the Glasgow & South Western Railway opened a rail link between Johnstone and Princes Pier, Greenock, thereby offering an alternative route to Glasgow. The G&SWR did not own ships in its own right until 1888. The pier and railway station were rebuilt and extended between 1892 and 1894 at a cost of over £62,000. A principal feature of the new buildings were the four Italianate towers constructed of Ruabon red brick.

LLANDUDNO
PS Alexandra 1891 29434

By 1848 the London, Brighton & South Coast Railway were keen to promote Brighton as a cross-channel port; they funded the Brighton & Continental Steam Packet Co, though it was soon found that Newhaven on the Ouse was a far more practicable choice. In those days railway companies were forbidden from owning passenger ships without Parliamentary approval, a fact not lost on the LB&SCR's arch-rival the London & South Eastern. Within months the LB&SCR were in court, found guilty, and heavily fined. They were now in a catch-22 situation. As the B&CSPCo had been adjudged a wholly-owned subsidiary, there was the certainty of further heavy fines if it continued to operate, and the railway's directors would be imprisoned for contempt of court. Unable to function, the B&CSPCo had no way of raising revenue or finance to pay back the funding and become independent. The line ceased trading (but was not liquidated) and its three paddlers sold. The railway then entered into an arrangement with Maple & Morris. The latter would own and manage steamers for a Newhaven-Dieppe service, but the railway would operate them and timetable trains so as to connect with arrivals and departures. In 1863, railway companies were at last given powers to own their own passenger ships. With some thousands of pounds in the kitty from the B&CSPCo fiasco, the iron-hulled paddler 'Alexandra' was ordered from Cairn & Co, Greenock.

In 1883 she was sold to the Plymouth Promenade Pier Co, but worked excursion traffic around the Bristol Channel. Under their ownership she was refitted, being given a forward sun deck and an alley-wayed saloon aft. She was later sold to R & D Jones, Liverpool, for excursion work along the North Wales coast, and it was whilst she was in their ownership that she was photographed here off Little Orme Head in 1891. The following year she was sold to James Jones of Swansea, and operated out of Milford Haven. She had a further refit in 1893 which included reboilering and the fitting of new compound engines. In 1895 she was sold yet again, this time to the Hastings & St Leonard's Steam Boat Co for work along the south coast. She was broken up in 1905.

GRAVESEND, THE FERRY 1902 49044A

The Tilbury-Gravesend ferry service was operated by the London, Tilbury & Southend Railway. When the LT&SR was absorbed into the Midland Railway in 1912, there were four ferries on the service: the 'Rose' (built 1901), the 'Catherine' (1903), the 'Gertrude' (1906) and the recently-completed 'Edith'. All were twin-screw vessels of less than 300 grt. The 'Gertrude' was sold in 1932, and the others were replaced by motor vessels between late 1960 and mid 1961.

BRIGHTON 1902 48508

In 1887 Peter and Alexander Campbell decided to relocate their excursion steamer business from Scotland to the relatively untapped Bristol Channel, where they soon came to dominate the market. In 1901 they expanded operations to the south coast when they bought the Brighton, Worthing & South Coast Steamboat Co. At the beginning of the 20th century, Brighton was the most popular seaside resort in Britain, and Campbells could, and did, reinforce their Brighton fleet when necessary by transferring steamers from the Bristol Channel. This allowed them to corner the bulk of excursions out of Brighton and Eastbourne, and to gain a substantial foothold in the Isle of Wight and Hastings traffic.

WEYMOUTH
The Jersey Boat 1898 41127

The Great Western Railway ordered two fast triple-expansion steamers, costing £55,000 each, from the Naval Construction & Armaments Co, Barrow-in-Furness, for the Weymouth-Jersey summer service. At 1186 grt, 'Roebuck' carried 487 first- and 240 third-class passengers. Her first duty was to carry the GWR directors and guests to the Spithead Naval Review in June 1897, entering revenue-earning service one week later. In January 1905, whilst laid up at Milford for the winter, she caught fire and sank under the weight of hose water in her hull. Raised, she was taken to Barrow for a refit and was back in time for the commencement of the summer service. 'Roebuck' was in trouble again in July 1911 when she ran aground on Kaines Reef, St Brelades. Eventually patched up and refloated, she was heading for St Helier accompanied by the tug 'Em.Z.Sviter' when water started pouring into her. Beached to save her from sinking, she was again patched up and taken to Harland & Wolff, Southampton for repairs. Requisitioned for minesweeping duties during the Great War, she became a casualty in the Orkneys on 13 January 1915, when she parted her moorings during a gale and finished up impaled upon the ram bow of the depot ship HMS 'Imperieuse', sinking in shallow water. Her sister ship, 'Reindeer' (1193 grt), entered service on 3 August 1897, and one month later, whilst entering Weymouth, she succeeded in ramming the Bournemouth & South Coast SPCo's 'Brodick Castle'. Requisitioned for minesweeping duties in October 1914, she was sent to the Mediterranean, where on the night of 6 June 1915, whilst travelling without lights, she rammed and sank the 'Immingham'. After the war she was refitted and returned to service with the GWR, with whom she remained until sold for breaking up in December 1928.

Weymouth 1898 41112

Here we see paddlers belonging to the Weymouth, Bournemouth & Swanage Steam Packet Co with the 'Premier' nearest the camera and the 'Victoria' behind her. The livery is black hull and funnel with white saloons and paddle-boxes. This was changed in 1901 to black hull (white above sponson level), buff funnel with a black top, and white saloons and paddle-boxes.

Weymouth, The Jersey Boat 1890 27318

A boat from Jersey enters Weymouth, whilst over on the left a paddler makes ready to depart. On the right, just peeping from behind the harbour wall, is what might be the paddler 'Great Western'. She had either just been, or was about to be sold to Nathaniel Miller for his Preston-Dublin service. 'Great Western' was built in 1867 by Simons & Co, Renfrew, for the Milford-Cork service operated by Ford & Jackson, but was taken over by the GWR in 1872. In the 1880s she had been chartered to the Weymouth & Channel Islands Steam Packet Co.

LULWORTH COVE 1894 34570

The WB&SSPCo paddler 'Victoria' disembarks trippers on to the steep-shelved beach in Lulworth Cove. Built of steel in 1884 by J & K Smit, Kinderdijk, and engined by Penn & Sons, London, 'Victoria' had specially-strengthened bows to allow her to run on to shingle beaches. This was not as straightforward as it might sound. The ship approached the beach at right angles, dropping a stern anchor. As soon as she grounded, the slack in the anchor cable was taken up and this held her bows on to the beach. 'Victoria' was lengthened in 1888 and reboilered in 1912. Her bell-topped funnel was replaced a few years after this picture was taken. She survived until January 1953, when she proceeded under her own steam to the breaker's yard.

◆

POOLE
The Swanage Boat 1908 61183
Here we see the paddle steamer 'Brodick Castle' at Weymouth
quayside. She was built in 1878 for service in Scotland. In 1886
the Bournemouth, Swanage and Poole Steam Packet Company
lost their new steamer ' Bournemouth' in fog, when she was
wrecked on Portland Bill. They purchased 'Brodick Castle' as a
replacement. In 1901 the vessel was sold to Cosens & Co of
Weymouth, who were the owners when this picture was taken.
She was sold for service in Buenos Aires in 1909, but foundered
under tow during the delivery voyage.

—◆—

St Helier, SS Gazelle 1893 31629

In 1889 the Great Western Railway took over the Weymouth & Channel Islands Steam Packet Co, immediately ordering three new ships, 'Lynx', 'Antelope' and 'Gazelle', from Laird Bros, Birkenhead. To save time, an off-the-shelf Laird's design was chosen; the three-ship deal cost the GWR £100,000. They were to be the first triple-expansion twin-screw packets to operate scheduled services in the English Channel. 'Antelope' and 'Lynx' were delivered in July 1889, 'Gazelle' at the beginning of September. All three had interesting and varied careers. On 10 June 1890 'Antelope' was holed on Cavale Rocks, Guernsey; during a gale in November 1893 she ran out of coal, but managed to get into shelter in Swanage Bay where she was refuelled. On 5 September 1890, 'Lynx' was rammed by the tanker 'Oevelgonne', which did not stop - she was subsequently arrested on a visit to Falmouth. During the Great War, both 'Lynx' and 'Gazelle' served as Royal Navy minesweepers, 'Gazelle' taking part in the Dardanelles campaign. 'Antelope' had been sold in 1913, but by March 1920 the surviving sisters were back on station for the GWR, though both were used for cargo runs only. 'Lynx' made her final run to Jersey in March 1925; she then sailed for Plymouth, where she was laid up. 'Gazelle' followed a few weeks later, and both were sold for scrap the following September.

FLEETWOOD
PS Mona's Queen 1904 52171
The Isle of Man Steam Packet Co's 'Mona's Queen'
eases out of Fleetwood on a summer sailing. During
the Great War the paddler was employed on
trooping duties across the Channel. At about
2315hrs on 6 February 1917, whilst carrying troops
between Southampton and Havre, she rammed a
German U-boat. The U-boat might well have been
travelling along with only its conning tower
showing above the surface, as it was pushed under
by her port paddle-wheel. The submarine then
sank by the bow, its stern lifting clear of the water.
On arrival back at Southampton, her paddle-box
was found to be damaged and she was sent to
Harland & Wolff for repairs.

FLEETWOOD
SS Viking 1908 59939
The IOMSPCo turbine-steamer 'Viking' departs for Douglas. When this picture was taken, the IOMSPCo and Midland Railway Co turbine-steamers were usually assigned to the Liverpool-Douglas and Heysham-Douglas routes. It was also possible to sail to Douglas from Barrow, Silloth, Whitehaven and Glasgow. The crossing from Fleetwood took about three hours; the daily sailing was scheduled to leave after the arrival of the 1415hrs train. There was also a twice-weekly sailing from here to Ramsey via Douglas.

FLEETWOOD, PS PHILOMEL 1908 59940

The Furness Railway paddle-steamer 'Philomel' is entering Fleetwood. Built in 1899 for the General Steam Navigation Co, the paddler was purchased by the Furness Railway in 1907 and entered service on the Barrow-Fleetwood run in April 1908.

BELFAST, THE GLASGOW BOAT 1897 40233

The last of the transatlantic paddle-liners, Cunard's 'Scotia', was finally withdrawn in September 1875, while the last transpacific paddler managed to linger on for another six years. In Britain, paddlers still found favour with cross-channel and excursion steamer operators, and new tonnage would continue to be built well into the 20th century. In the late 1880s, cross-channel paddlers were capable of service speeds of up to 20 knots, and in 1893 the Belgian Marine Administration's 'Marie Henriette' attained 22.2 knots on her trials.

BELFAST

SS Dynamic 1896 40230

Commanded by Capt J T Ross, the Belfast Steamship Company's express passenger steamship SS 'Dynamic' carries the Belfast Harbour Commissioners on their annual inspection in 1896. The late-1870s saw a period of intense competition on the Irish Sea ferry services, forcing the BSC to modernise its fleet; the 'Semaphore' underwent a major refit that included lengthening her hull and reboilering her, and she was then renamed 'Telegraphic'. Two other ships were sold, releasing funds to allow BSC to order the 'Dynamic' from Harland & Wolff - she was the first vessel to be built at the Queen's Island Shipyard, and the last in the BSC fleet with an iron hull. When completed, 'Dynamic' was the fastest steamship on the Irish Sea. Because of her speed, she was chartered by the Admiralty during 1885-86; she was then given a refit and had electricity installed. On 3 January 1891, the 'Manchester', a steamship belonging to a rival company, left Belfast for Liverpool. One hour later the 'Dynamic' sailed from Prince's Dock, also bound for Liverpool. Her turn of speed was such that she was able to catch up with the 'Manchester' and berth at Liverpool at approximately the same time. Stiff competition meant that these ships were rarely idle. When not on scheduled crossings, they would be used on Saturday excursions from Belfast. A typical excursion would be to Largs and back at 2s 6d for saloon and 1s 6d for steerage passengers. On-board entertainment was usually provided by a band, including regimental bands from units of the British Army stationed in Ireland. By the late 1890s, however, 'Dynamic' was getting past her best. Her iron hull would soon need a considerable amount of money to be spent on it if she was to maintain her status as a fast ship. It was decided that the expense would be too much, and in 1901 she was sold.

◆

BELFAST
The Douglas Boat 1897 40232
Passengers on a Douglas boat take in the sights, sounds and smells
of Belfast Harbour. Amongst the companies operating services to
Belfast were the IOMSPCo, the Barrow Steam Navigation Co,
controlled by the Midland Railway with sailings from Barrow and
Morecambe, and a joint Lancashire & Yorkshire and London &
North Western Railway service from Fleetwood. In 1900 the
Midland Railway began to develop Heysham as a cross-channel
port, ordering four new steamers for the route. They were of a
similar size at around the 2000 grt mark and about 340 ft in length,
and each were able to carry 2000 passengers. The main difference
was that two were twin-screw triple-expansion, and two were triple-
screw direct turbine ships. When the turbine ships began running
in 1904, they were the first of their type to visit Belfast.

DUBLIN
Kingstown 1897 39308

Kingstown was the Irish terminal of the City of Dublin Steam Packet Co, who successfully operated the mail service between Holyhead and Dublin for several decades. Between 1860 and 1896 the route was operated by the fast four-funnelled paddle-steamers 'Ulster', 'Munster', 'Leinster' and 'Connaught', which were contracted under penalty clauses to make the crossing in no more than 3.75 hours. The daily schedule required two ships on the run, each making two round trips, with a third in steam on standby able to sail at immediate notice. The remaining unit of the quartet would usually be undergoing general maintenance or even a refit. Though rebuilt in the 1880s, the paddlers were replaced in the 1890s by four Laird-built twin-screw, four-cylinder triple-expansion steamers, each of about 2600 grt. In this picture one of the new steamers is alongside the pier. If the date of the picture is correct, the large paddler might be the 'Ireland'. She was built in 1885 as cover for the Provinces as they were rebuilt in turn, emerging with new engines and two funnels.

◆

DUBLIN

NORTH WALL 1897 39282
From 1862 North Wall was the
Dublin terminus for London &
North Western Railway steamers
from Holyhead. For years the
LNWR did its best to wrest the
lucrative Irish Mail sea-passage
contract from the clutches of the
CofDSPCo, but it was not until the
commissioning of the 'Shamrock'
and the 'Banshee' in the 1870s
that they had ships to match the
speed of the CofDSPCo ships.
Even then, they failed to secure
the contract.

DUBLIN 1897 39283
A number of scheduled steamer services linked Dublin to England and Scotland. Among the daily services were those to Glasgow (18 hours; the fare was 15s), Liverpool (fares 7s and 13s 6d) and Holyhead. There were twice-weekly sailings to places such as Plymouth (15s and 20s), Falmouth and Southampton.

Around the Ports & Harbours

PERCH ROCK LIGHTHOUSE 1887 20069
The Black Rock had long been a hazard to navigation for ships entering or leaving Liverpool. There were various attempts at providing a light, but it was not until the 1820s that a substantial stone-built lighthouse was erected. It was built at a cost of £27,000. Excluding the lantern, the lighthouse rises 90ft; the first 36ft is solid granite held together with puzzolana, a volcanic sand that sets immensely strongly when mixed with lime. The revolving light was made by Robinson & Wilson of London, and cost £2300 including machinery. Warning is given by a white light flashing once every twenty seconds and visible at 14 miles in clear weather. During daylight hours, when the depth of water in Rock Gut is less than eleven feet, a black ball is exhibited by the side of the lantern. During the hours of darkness the same message is conveyed by means of a fixed white light.

FORT PERCH ROCK 1887 20067
Designed by Capt John Kitson, Royal Engineers, Fort Perch Rock
was built between 1826 and 1829 at a cost of £27,000 to defend the
seaward approach to Liverpool and the Mersey. Its construction was
first proposed during the Napoleonic Wars, but it was delayed as
Liverpool Corporation and the Board of Ordnance attempted to
out-smart one another into picking up the bill. Because a lighthouse
was also being proposed, it appears that the Corporation was
hoping that the Army would pay for both by building a fort that
incorporated a lighthouse. Not to be outdone, the Army did its best
to convince the Corporation that they should build a lighthouse
that could double up as a coastal artillery platform. After the fort
was completed, local fishermen found that they could earn
themselves a few pounds by recovering cannon balls fired during
gunnery drill and then selling them back to the Army.

LIVERPOOL
SS Adriatic 1890 24417
Here we see the White Star liner 'Adriatic' in the Mersey. Built
by Harland & Wolff, Belfast, she was launched in October 1871
and made her maiden voyage to New York in April 1872. A few
weeks later, she lifted the record for the westbound crossing of
the Atlantic from Cunard's 'Scotia' with a speed of 14.52 knots.
When built she carried 50 first- and 800 third-class passengers.
In the 1890s a number of liners operated by either White Star,
Cunard, Canadian Pacific or P&O were considered by the
Admiralty as suitable for arming as merchant cruisers should
the need arise. The 1893 list included six White Star vessels:
'Majestic', 'Teutonic', 'Britannic', 'Germanic', 'Celtic' and
'Adriatic'. The owners received an annual subsidy towards the
first two, but not the others.

LIVERPOOL, SS CITY OF PARIS 1890 25083

The Inman Line was one of the principal players on the North Atlantic service, holding mail contracts for Liverpool to New York and Liverpool to Halifax. By the late 1870s, the line was facing tough competition from Cunard, White Star, Dominion, and the Guion Line; Inman's problems were further compounded in 1881 with the loss of the 'City of Brussels' and the failure of the new 'City of Rome' to live up to expectations. The Inman specification for the latter called not only for the finest in passenger comfort and accommodation, but for a ship fast enough to regain and hold the transatlantic record. After six round trips, the fastest passage made by 'City of Rome' was still seven hours slower than the existing record. Inman returned her to her builders accompanied by a claim for £140,000. Owing to over-capacity of the route Inman went into voluntary liquidation in 1886, but was immediately taken over by the American-financed International Steamship Co and was reborn as the Inman & International Line. The new company immediately ordered two new liners: the magnificent, record-breaking, twin screw 'City of Paris' and 'City of New York'. Despite this, the line was still beset with problems. In 1887 'City of Montreal' was lost by fire at sea. In 1891 'City of Paris' suffered major damage to her engine room as a result of her starboard shaft breaking, and the following year 'City of Chicago' was wrecked off Ireland. The last I & I sailing took place in 1893; the four surviving ships in the fleet were transferred to the American Line, earning their keep on the US mail run between New York and Southampton.

By the time Inman's 'City of Paris' was built at J & G Thompsons (later John Brown & Co), passenger comfort on the transatlantic route had come a long way since the pioneering days of the 'Royal William', the 'Sirius' and the 'Great Western' in the 1830s. Both Isambard Kingdom Brunel and Samuel Cunard were quick to realise that there was a market where comfort equalled ticket sales. Brunel's 'Great Britain' was the first liner equipped with proper lavatories; until then, one of the more onerous tasks facing the cabin steward was to empty the passengers' chamber-pots every morning. When he designed the 'Great Eastern' for the Australia run, Brunel made it a feature that even her smallest cabin was twice the size of the largest cabin on any other liner afloat, and that they were fitted with wash basins and hot and cold running water. Not all innovation was British-led. The American Collins Line were the first to fit their ships with ice rooms, enabling all manner of foods to be served during the passage. They were also the first line to provide cabins with steam heating and bathrooms.

'City of Paris' could accommodate 540 1st-class, 200 2nd-class and 1000 steerage passengers in varying degrees of comfort. These differences reflected the subtle changes that were occurring in passenger loadings; more and more wealthy Americans became not only keen to visit Europe, but expected to travel across the pond in the very best ▶

of accommodation, eating haute cuisine food and drinking the very finest of wines. As shipping lines tried to out-do one another, offering the very best of comfort combined with fast crossing times, transatlantic liners soon went from being sea-going first-class hotels to floating palaces. The lot of the steerage passengers also improved. They might not figure in the order of things should it come to allocating places in the lifeboats, but at least their somewhat Spartan accommodation was clean, they had proper lavatories and washing facilities, and they no longer had to provide their own food.

LIVERPOOL, SS CITY OF PARIS 1890 25088

LIVERPOOL, SS CITY OF PARIS 1890 25087

LIVERPOOL

St George's Dock c1881 14149

Construction of St George's Dock was authorised by an Act of Parliament in 1761. The
town's third dock, it extended from the corner of St Nicholas Churchyard to Moor Street;
the land was provided by the Corporation. The decision to build St George's was one of
necessity, as the Old Dock, prone to silting, had to be closed on occasion for dredging, while
the Salthouse Dock, completed in 1748, was already too small to take the larger merchant
ships then being built. When originally built, St George's Dock covered just over 20,000 sq
yds and had a total quayage of 700 yds. It was linked to the town's two older docks and the
graving dock, allowing vessels to move between them without having to enter the Mersey. St
George's was later enlarged to 31,000 sq yds and linked to Prince's Dock. When it was
eventually filled in, the site of the dock was occupied by the headquarters of the Mersey
Docks & Harbour Board, the Cunard Building and the Royal Liver Insurance Building.

◆

RUNCORN
The Docks c1900 R67301

The construction of the Manchester Ship Canal resulted in access to Runcorn Docks having to be made by way of locks opposite the town's waterfront, or through the Eastham Locks. By far the most important trade at Runcorn was china clay from Devon and Cornwall, bound for the Potteries. Most of the clay came from Fowey, Par or Charlestown; the traffic remained one of the last strongholds of coastal merchant sailing ships well into the 20th century. Runcorn was also a coal port, handling traffic from Lancashire and Staffordshire pits. Seasonal traffic included cargoes of fish in May and June, bound for the curing houses of Stornoway, Peterhead and Wick.

**LIVERPOOL, THE CUSTOMS HOUSE
1887** 20015

Liverpool's fifth Customs House was
built on the site of the Old Dock and
opened in 1839. During the 18th
century, Liverpool merchants were
practised in the noble arts of customs
evasion, especially the royal duty due
on tobacco. By falsifying the allowances
for repacking imported tobacco, and by
not surrendering all the damaged
tobacco to be burnt, a merchant could
make a handsome additional return on
his investment. Things came to a head
in 1706 when the Excise launched a full
investigation of the port over alleged
customs avoidance.

MANCHESTER SHIP CANAL 1895 36396
The MSC, some 36 miles in length, was one of the great civil engineering projects of the late 19th century; it was completed in 1894 at a cost of £14.3 million. Construction began in 1887. It involved the excavation and removal of 48 million cubic yds of earth, the building of a tidal lock at Eastham, and of four other sets of locks to raise the canal sixty feet above sea level at Manchester. Construction work also used up 70 million bricks and 750,000 tons of granite, and at its height employed over 16,000 workers.

MANCHESTER SHIP CANAL 1894 33810
During its first year of operations the MSC handled
exports totalling 299,407 tons and imports of 386,751
tons; in 1897 the figures rose to 494,862 tons and
1,053,637 tons respectively. With the mills of Oldham
and Bolton preferring to use Egyptian rather than
American cotton, the MSC saw its share of total UK
imports for Egyptian cotton rise from 21.4 per cent
during 1895-1896 to 33.6 per cent by 1899-1900; in
anticipation of lucrative contracts for frozen meat, the
MSC went ahead in 1895 with the construction of cold
storage buildings at Manchester. Manchester also had its
own shipping companies. James Knott founded Port
Line in 1894, offering a direct service to Alexandria,
which was in direct competition with the Liverpool-
based Moss Line. Knott was helped by the MSC, who
gave his ships free towage, discounted dock labour, and
provided free barging of cargo to and from Liverpool.
Manchester Liners was registered in May 1898; its
intention was to operate services to and from Canada.
Their first cargo to arrive in Manchester was aboard the
Raylton Dixon-built 'Manchester City' (5833 grt). It
included 450 head of cattle, 150 sheep, 67,000 bushels
of maize, 39,929 bushels of wheat, and 37,117 bushels
and 1500 bags of oats. The bulk of the cargo was within
carting distance of the docks.

MANCHESTER SHIP CANAL 1894 33697
This steamer has just passed through Latchford Locks. The course
of the canal meant that a section of the L&NWR line to Liverpool
via Warrington and Speke would have to be re-routed; this resulted
in the building of Latchford Viaduct. It was completed in 1893, but
was used for freight only; passenger trains continued to use the
original route until the last possible moment. Beyond the viaduct is
the Knutsford Road Swingbridge and the Latchford High Level
Bridge. This was the last section of canal to be completed; the
excavation was 55ft deep.

PRESTON DOCKS 1893 33097

Situated on the navigable Ribble, Preston Docks opened in 1892. In the 1890s
the scheduled cargo service between Preston and Belfast was handled by just one
ship, the 417 grt 'Helen Craig', built in 1891 by Workman Clarke & Co for the
Belfast & Preston Transport Co. She came equipped with a towing hook, so that
if she came across any of the company's schooners becalmed, she could take
them in tow. Perhaps the longest-serving member of her crew was John Kennedy.
He joined her as a seaman in 1893 and retired as her skipper in 1949. 'Helen
Craig' steamed on until 1959, when she was sold for breaking up. She was given
a civic send-off from Preston as she sailed out for the last time.

FLEETWOOD HARBOUR 1894 33968

Fleetwood was founded in 1836 by Sir Peter Hesketh-Fleetwood, and laid out to the designs of Decimus Burton, who designed the North Euston Hotel, Queen's Terrace and both lighthouses. They planned that the town would be a little way inland and separate from the dock area. For a short time Fleetwood was in effect the northern terminus of the L&NWR line from Euston, and the connecting stop for steamer services to and from Belfast, Ardrossan and various west coast ports. The railway reached Fleetwood in July 1840, six years before Blackpool. The line was single-track and ran from Preston via Kirkham, Poulton and Thornton. Fleetwood lacked the infrastructure to compete with Liverpool as a major port for passenger and cargo traffic, but it did become England's principal fishing port on the west coast with a fleet to rival those of Hull and Grimsby. The advantages that Fleetwood had as a port were that its entrance channel was free of hazards to navigation, such as sand bars and moving banks. Even at low tide, vessels drawing less than sixteen feet of water could manoeuvre within the harbour basin, and boats drawing less than five feet could still use the channel. In this picture there are trawlers and Morecambe Bay prawners. Average dimensions for the trawlers were 60ft x 16.8ft x 9.5ft. Carvel built, they had an oak keel and frames and pine planking. Usually crewed by four men and a boy, and capable of staying at sea for about six days, they operated throughout Liverpool Bay, Cardigan Bay and around the Isle of Man, trawling for plaice, sole, haddock, and cod. The Morecambe Bay prawner, also known locally as a half-decker, shrimper, or nobby, was a cutter-rigged smack varying in length from about 23ft to 40ft. They were fast and possessed excellent sea-keeping qualities. Usually crewed by a man and a boy, they trawled at between six and fifteen fathoms. The prawner was popular with fishermen from the Solway Firth to North Wales.

DOUGLAS HARBOUR 1893 32995A

Here we see IOMSPCo paddlers at Douglas in 1893; by this time the number of annual visitors coming to the island was fast approaching the 400,000 mark. Regular steamship services between Douglas and Liverpool were begun in 1822 by the St George Steam Packet Co. Though the summer service was adequate, winter sailings appear to have been sporadic. West coast steamship companies may have been either unable or unwilling to provide the level of year-round services that Man required; a direct result of this was the formation of the Manx-owned Mona's Isle Company in December 1829. The StGSPCo retaliated by starting a price war, and soon both companies were slashing fares; the lowest ever advertised by the StGSPCo was just 6d each way. The StGSPCo also transferred their fast steamer 'St George' from their Irish route to the Isle of Man run in the hope of speeding up the crossing time between Douglas and Liverpool, but unfortunately she was wrecked on Conister Rock a few weeks later, having lost her cable whilst attempting to ride out a storm. In July 1831 the StGSPCo threw in the towel and abandoned services to Man. In 1832 the Mona's Isle Co changed its name to the Isle of Man United Steam Packet Co and bought a second vessel. Three years later the company changed its name once more by dropping the United from of its title. Over the next hundred and fifty years, the IOMSPCo would not only play a major role in the development of the Island, but also its ships would serve with distinction in two world wars.

◆

DOUGLAS
Victoria Pier 1907 59160A

Ship-handling facilities at Douglas were greatly
improved in 1872 with the completion of Victoria
Pier, as it allowed steamers to come alongside
regardless of the state of the tide. By this date the
number of annual visitors had broken the 100,000
barrier and was still climbing. In order to increase
capacity, the pier was extended in 1888 to a length
of 1620ft. By the summer season of 1907, turbine-
steamers such as the Midland Railway's 'Manxman'
were bringing 2000 passengers per trip. The two
small ferries berthed in front of the IOMSPCo
paddler are the 'Rose' and the 'Thistle'. They were
used to transfer people to and from Douglas Head.
Note the advertisements on their sterns.

DOUGLAS BAY
The Tower of Refuge 1893 33007

It could be said that the life of Sir William Hillary (1771-1847) was the stuff of ripping yarns. A knight of St John of Jerusalem, soldier, author and philanthropist, he was also a suspected bigamist, who settled in the Isle of Man in order to put a few miles and a little water between himself and his creditors, and to bury quietly the murkier details surrounding his elopement and marriage to his wife. At this date there were few lifeboats in service around Britain's coast, and no umbrella organisation to oversee things. Sir William served as a crew member of the Douglas lifeboat, and in 1824 became the principal founder of what would become the RNLI. In 1832 he built the Tower of Refuge on Conister Rock as a shelter for mariners unfortunate enough to be shipwrecked there. During his service with the Douglas lifeboat, Sir William assisted in the rescue of over 500 people, and on one occasion continued to help with a rescue despite having sustained six fractured ribs. Sir William died in 1847 and was buried in St George's churchyard, Douglas. Even in death he was still pursued by his creditors. They dug up his body and sold it for dissection.

◆

ROTHESAY PIER 1900 45990
Rothesay developed as a holiday and tourist destination during the 1840s, attracting the opening of hotels, lodging houses, cafes and restaurants. The pier buildings were erected in 1882, though a plan to replace them in the late 1930s was dropped on the outbreak of war.

HELENSBURGH

The Empress 1901 47416

A former warship, the 'Empress', rides at anchor off Gareloch, where she was stationed for many years as an Industrial Training Ship for homeless and destitute boys. There were a number of these ships at various locations, including the 'Mount Edgcumbe' (ex HMS 'Winchester') at Saltash. 'Empress' was not the only wooden wall in Scottish waters. The 46-gun frigate HMS 'Unicorn', laid down during the Napoleonic Wars, was still building when hostilities ceased. Building work continued after a fashion, and she was finally launched in 1824, whereupon she went immediately into reserve at Chatham. Later she served as a floating gunpowder store at Woolwich before being selected for conversion into a drill ship. On 1 January 1874, fifty years after she was launched, 'Unicorn' was finally commissioned as a RNR drill ship at Dundee.

◆

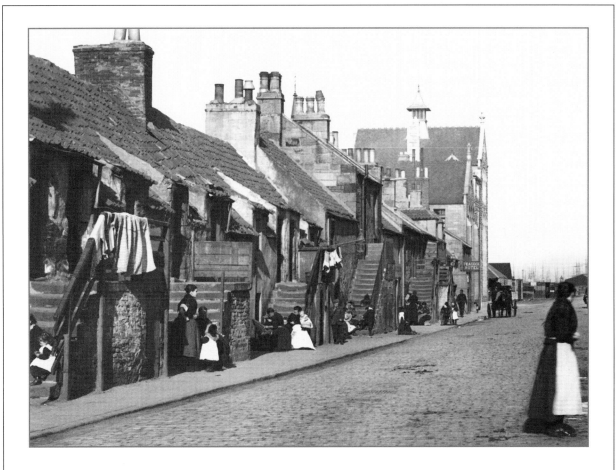

NEWHAVEN
Fishermen's Cottages 1897 39137
These cottages at Newhaven, Fife, are an example of the types
of fishermen's dwelling that could be found around harbours
from Scotland to at least Cullercoats in Northumbria, usually
single-story terraces with slate or stone roofing. On the west
coast of England, the old fishing communities tended to be
housed in cottages with thatched roofs. At Newhaven the
fishermen's wives were noted for the way they dressed, which
was said to reflect the community's Dutch and Scandinavian
origins, and for their cries when selling fish: 'caller herrin'
(fresh herrings) and 'caller ou' (fresh oysters).

HARTLEPOOL 1903 49993

The crews of the fishing boats prepare to hoist sail once they have cleared Hartlepool. The paddler giving them a tow is an example of what had become the classic design for this type of vessel: a tall funnel immediately abaft of two large paddle-boxes. Her power plant would be a one- or two-cylinder half side-lever steam engine, the cylinder(s) mounted vertically, which meant that the piston rods drove upwards. Among the paddle-tugs working on the Tees in 1903 were the 'Sir Joseph Pease', built in 1896, and the 'Isaac Wilson' and 'Salt', both of 1889.

HULL, ALEXANDRA DOCK 1903 49825

Steamers discharge their cargo by way of chutes into dumb barges. In the centre of the picture is a Humber keel, sporting the traditional rig of a single square lug sail. Behind her is a small steam tug which was making ready to tow several barges down the Trent to Nottingham. The steamer in the background is the locally-built (1896) and registered 'Dido'.

HULL, PRINCES DOCK 1903 49824
The Humber keel on the left carries a foresail, an indication that she is sloop-rigged. We can see her pronounced stem and above that the hawse timber, which may or may not be sporting a small carving. On each side of the hawse timber are a number of wooden stanchions called timber heads, which were used to secure her when mooring. We can also see her handspike-operated winch, an aid to raising anchor in tidal waters.

HULL, THE PIER 1903 49820
Passengers have plenty to look at whilst they await the arrival of their ferry. A steamer rides at anchor awaiting a tug to take her into Hull, while another is just about to enter the port complex. The paddler on the right is the ferry 'Atalanta'.

HULL
The Pier 1903 49821

There are plenty of spectators on the pier to watch the arrival at
Hull of the Eclipse class cruiser HMS 'Dido'. Built in 1896 by the
London & Glasgow Shipbuilding Co, 'Dido' displaced 5600 tons
and was armed with 5 x 6-inch and 7 x 4.7-inch guns. The class was
re-armed in 1905-06 to mount 11 x 6-inch, 8 x 12-pdr (12 cwt), 1 x
12-pdr (8 cwt), 7 x 3-pdr, 2 Maxims and 3 x 18-inch torpedo tubes
(including one stern tube). Powered by two sets of inverted triple
expansion engines, fed by eight boilers and 24 furnaces, the
Eclipses could exceed 19-20 knots for short periods. Riding at
anchor to the right of the funnel of the 'Manchester' is HMS
'Southampton', a boys' training ship at Hull from 1867 to 1912.

GRIMSBY, THE DOCKS 1893 33272

Amid this forest of masts and spars are the three-masted barque 'Warden Law', the three-masted barquentine 'Violet', and the two-masted schooner 'Pride of Anglesey'. Nearer the camera is a Humber keel, and alongside her is the ketch-rigged Yorkshire billieboy 'Tiger'.

GRIMSBY, THE DOCKS 1893 33273

There was a time in the 19th century when the powers that be in Hull looked upon the needs of the fishing industry as little more than a nuisance and a hindrance to commercial traffic. Not so Grimsby, where facilities were improved, and Hull trawler owners were offered inducements to cross the river. By 1891 the Grimsby fleet numbered 800 sail and 35 steam vessels; yet by the beginning of the 20th century it had changed to 500 steam and 34 large sailing trawlers.

GRIMSBY, ALEXANDRA DOCK 1904 51829
Here we see loaded barges and empty Humber keels. Of the latter, the one nearest the camera on the extreme right looks very much the worse for wear. The keel next in line carries the top and mainsail rig of a Sheffield-size craft, while the third keel is sloop-rigged.

BOSTON, DOUGHTY QUAY 1890 26066
The paddle-tug 'Boston' was built at South Shields in 1875 for the Boston Steam Tug Co. She had a wooden clinker-built hull and was powered by a grasshopper engine. Her steering position was on the main deck foreword of the bridge. As well as for towing, she was used on excursion work.

BOSTON, THE DOCKS 1893 32078

Of interest here is the single-hold steam coaster, one of hundreds of such vessels in the 90ft to 140ft range, which were capable of carrying up to about 300 tons of cargo into the smallest of harbours. Many were employed on scheduled feeder runs between small harbours and the big ports; others traded in the 'go anywhere for any cargo' world of tramping. It has been estimated that prior to the outbreak of the Great War about half of Britain's coastal fleet was engaged in the transport of coal.

KINGS LYNN 1898 40893

The Great Ouse, navigable for over 75 miles from Bedford to the Wash, flows through Kings Lynn. The docks are situated about two miles inland at Vinegar Middle Sand, and in the late 18th century were ranked fifth most important in England. Once a whaling port, Kings Lynn in the late 19th century was handling coal from the North East and grain, and had a small inshore fishing fleet.

GREAT YARMOUTH 1891 28699

Prior to the opening of the railways, considerable quantities of goods for Norwich and the villages along the way were sent up-river from Great Yarmouth. Much of it was carried by wherries, clinker-hulled double-ended barges, that carried a single loose footed gaff sail of about 1200 sq ft. They varied in length from about 55ft to over 60ft, and could carry 40 tons of cargo.

Several of them can be seen in this picture: the two in the background with white patches on their bows are North River wherries, which traded to places like North Walsham, but were limited because of depth of water to about 15 tons of cargo. Their masts were stepped so that they could pass under bridges.

LOWESTOFT HARBOUR 1887 19838A

In the 1880s the Lowestoft fishing fleet was dominated by two types of craft: gaff-rigged luggers
of around 65 ft in length and with a beam of 18ft, and 70ft ketch-rigged smacks. The luggers,
also known as dandies, drifted for herring and mackerel during the autumn and winter before
changing to a rig suitable for trawling during the summer months. The smacks were essentially
trawlers. A steam capstan was standard smack kit, used both for hauling the trawl and the
handling of sails. Halyards and sheets were connected to the capstan so that the skipper could
in effect sail her single-handed while his crew saw to the fish. From the mid 1890s a new class
of fishing vessel was introduced. These were smacks under 52 ft in length, known as toshers,
and were a way of circumventing regulations for the certification of skippers. The majority of
Lowestoft craft in the 1880s-90s appear to have been skipper-owned.

LONDON 1886 L130519

This is London in 1886, the year Tilbury opened some twenty miles down river. Beginning with the opening of the West India Dock in 1802, the 19th century saw London's docks transformed. Until then, ships carrying goods upon which customs duty had to be paid had to berth at the Legal Quays between London Bridge and the Tower. Coastal traffic upon which there were no customs dues discharged their cargoes along the Sufferance Wharfs on the south bank and at Wapping. Monopoly, corruption and vested interests saw to it that the Greenland Dock, Rotherhithe, and the Brunswick Dock, Blackwall, were prevented from being used as trading docks save for whaling. Ships often waited days for a berth, and even then might have to tie up five or six abreast. Note the lightermen rowing barges across the Pool. These are just a handful of the 3000 or so lighters and other small craft that worked the river.

ALDEBURGH, THE LIFEBOAT 1903 50426
In 1903 lifeboats were either of the pulling or sailing type. Steam power had been introduced into the RNLI in 1890 with the building of the 'Duke of Northumberland', but only five further examples were completed. In 1904 trials began of a lifeboat experimentally fitted with a petrol engine; this in turn led to the commissioning of the first custom-built motor lifeboat in 1908.

ROCHESTER 1894 34030
Here we see the three-masted barque 'Akarod'. By the 1890s it was not just the hulls of merchant sailing ships that were being constructed of iron or steel; many also carried steel masts, spars and fittings. Though there were many advantages, there was one great disadvantage, in that these vessels required shipyard facilities for refits and repairs; it was different in the days of wooden construction, when the crew would be capable of carrying out almost any type of repair, even a refit, themselves.

FOLKESTONE
The Harbour 1906 53473

In January 1899 the London Chatham & Dover Railway and the South Eastern Railway amalgamated their fleets under a joint management and operating agreement, though ownership remained unchanged. Folkestone harbour had been purchased by the SER in 1843, and was developed as a cross-channel port with services to and from Boulogne. The small paddler nearest the camera is the 'Myleta', one of two steel-hulled single-deck sister ships built for the SER in 1891 by Samuda Bros, Poplar. At 195 grt and powered by a two-cylinder simple engine, she was used on local services on the Medway, though from 1901 she was based at Ramsgate during the summer season for excursion traffic. Her small turtle weather forecastle was added after she entered service. Next to her is the somewhat larger 'Walmer', a twin-screw triple-expansion steamer built as the 'Trouville' for the LB&SCR by William Denny & Bros in 1894, and sold to the SE&CR in 1901. She was one of three sisters built for about £17,500 each for the Newhaven-Caen cargo service. However, the service proved to be unprofitable and was abandoned, and all three ships were sold to the SE&CR. The small steamer in the background could be either the 'Chatham' or the 'Roubaix' (ex 'Calais'). Both were iron-hulled cargo boats of less than 300 grt, built in the early 1870s by J & W Dudgeon, Cubitts Town, London, for the LC&DR to operate a six-days-a-week service between Dover and Calais. Both were transferred to the amalgamated fleet in 1901. 'Chatham' was sold for breaking up in September 1906. 'Roubaix' was sold to the LB&SCR in 1904 and renamed 'Trouville'. She was broken up in 1911.

RAMSGATE

THE HARBOUR 1901 48028

By the beginning of the 20th century, steam-powered drifters and trawlers were well-established in the UK fishing fleets. However, as can be seen here, sail would linger on in some areas for some time to come. In 1903 there were still 138 sailing smacks registered at Ramsgate, 193 at Brixham and no less than 356 at Lowestoft.

RYE 1901 47445

Rye sits huddled around a small hill, on the top of which stands St Mary's Church with its distinctive squat Norman tower. There was a time when Rye was considered important enough for it to be added to the original Cinque Ports along with Winchelsea. By 1901 Rye had long been surpassed as a port, though there were a number of lute-sterned trawlers based here, and cargoes arrived here for transfer into lighters that traded up the Rother as far as Bodiam. The Rother lighters were single-masted luggers, some of which had pointed sterns. Their main cargoes seem to have been coal, agricultural produce, timber, and shingle for road repairs. Bodiam Bridge, completed in 1796, marked the limit of normal navigation, but its centre arch was raised sufficiently to allow river traffic to continue upstream when conditions were favourable.

SOUTHAMPTON DOCKS 1908 60442

This was the port of destination or call for such lines as Union
Castle, North German Lloyd and American Lines. At noon every
Saturday an American Line liner left the Empress Dock bound for
New York. It was also from the Empress that the Cape Line mail
boats for South America and the West Indies departed. From the
Outer Dock there were services to the Channel Islands and
London (thrice weekly); there was a daily sailing to Le Havre, and
Tuesday, Thursday and Saturday departures for St Malo and
Cherbourg. Packets for Dublin, Falmouth, Plymouth, Glasgow,
Liverpool and Cork used the Town Pier, as did the ferry for Hythe,
while those for the Isle of Wight, Southsea and Portsmouth left
from the Royal Pier. Southampton came complete with dry docks,
graving docks and a foreign animals wharf.

◆

LYME REGIS
The Harbour 1892 31308

Lyme Regis harbour, or the Cobb, was once a seafaring settlement separate from the old town. The Cobb first enters recorded history in 1328, when Edward III granted it 'keyage' to the value of one penny in every pound for its maintenance. Lyme Regis is situated towards the northern end of Lyme Bay and six miles south of the mouth of the Axe, a river once navigable for some distance upstream. At Lyme there was a local variant of the Beer lugger. Slightly larger, but of the same basic design, these clinker-built open sailing boats were constructed so as to be able to cope with Lyme Bay's ground swell.

WEST BAY, THE QUAY 1897 40081

The brigantine lying in this Dorset harbour has a heavy transom counter, an indication that she might well be fifty years old or more. There were a number of developments in ship design during the 1830s to 1850s, partially influenced by new ways of measuring tonnage, that led to finer hull lines. It was also a period when wire shrouds began to replace thick hemp.

EXETER, THE DOCKS 1896 38037

The completion of Turf Lock in 1830 enabled vessels to enter the canal and proceed up to Exeter regardless of the state of the tide; the maximum dimensions possible were 122ft x 25ft x 10.5ft. Exeter was also the administrative centre for a part of the coast, with Sidmouth and Beer coming under its jurisdiction. The result was that between 1869 and 1880 around 800 fishing boats carried Exeter registrations.

EXETER

The Docks 1896 38036

Exeter City Basin opened in 1830 as the final stage of a canal
development going back to 1563. It was in that year that the city's
wool merchants, eager for more profits, commissioned John
Trew to make the Exe navigable to the estuary. However, Trew
came up with a different scheme, one that would overcome
expensive dredging operations, and the problems caused by
several weirs that had been built down-river. He proposed to
build a canal 1.75 miles in length and deep enough to allow
barges of up to 16 tons to dock at the city wharf at the watergate.
The transfer of goods between barges and sea-going ships would
take place in the estuary, thus cutting out both the middlemen at
Topsham and the need for packhorse trains.

SALCOMBE

The Quayside 1896 38483

In 1811 the local boat builder at Salcombe completed the
ketch 'Ceres' for Capt William Lewis of Bude for trading
with north Spanish ports, though for much of 1813 and 1814
she was employed carrying stores for Wellington's forces in
the Peninsular. In 1826 she was based at Bude; in 1852 she
was sold to Henry Petherick, whose family were to own her
until 1936. During the 1860s 'Ceres' was lengthened and her
cargo capacity raised to 85 tons, and in 1912 she was fitted
with a 30 hp semi-diesel engine. In November 1936 this 125-
year-old veteran was on passage from Swansea to Bude with a
cargo of slag, when her seams opened. She foundered off
Down End, Bideford Bay.

BIDEFORD
The Quay 1890 24800

Bideford was a busy little quay both for traffic up and down the Taw and Tamar rivers, and for general coasting trade between the north Devon and north Cornwall ports, the Bristol Channel and South Wales. As well as smack-rigged river barges, Bideford was home to a number of polacca brigantines, the smallest British square-rigged merchant sailing vessels. Crewed by three or four men, the polaccas varied in dimensions but were usually less than 70ft in length, with a beam of between 15ft and 19ft, and a draught when laden of between 8ft and 11ft. Though usually employed on coastal work, polaccas carried cargoes to and from the Mediterranean and Prince Edward Island. They were a hybrid design almost unique to Bideford. The pole foremast set a course and carried a topsail, and the mainmast sported a gaff mainsail and a gaff topsail. When grounded the polacca sat upright; this made it an ideal type of vessel for loading and unloading cargo on beaches at low water.

BRIXHAM 1896 38882

Brixham became a major fishing port ranking alongside Hull, Grimsby, Fleetwood, Lowestoft and Fraserburgh. It was from here that some of the biggest smack and ketch-rigged trawlers sailed to fish grounds ranging from the North Sea, the Irish Sea and the Western Approaches. The dimensions of these vessels varied, but many were around 80ft in length and registered at about 70 tons. They made full use of equipment such as steam capstans that considerably reduced the time it took to bring the trawl in. One custom observed by Brixham crews was no fishing on the Sabbath.

BRIXHAM 1889 21558

Smacks dry their sails within the protection of the outer harbour. These beam trawlers, so called because the trawl was kept open by a wooden beam across the mouth of the net, rarely ventured beyond the confines of the English Channel. They were noted as being fast sailers, and needed to be, as their catches often had to be landed in time to be loaded on to scheduled express fish trains.

DEVONPORT 1890 22462

Plymouth and Devonport were served by a number of ferries, including these wonderful steam-powered, chain-guided floating bridges on the Torpoint service, which were capable of carrying wheeled vehicles. Services operated were Ferry Road to Torpoint (fares 1d and 2d); the Barbican to Turnchapel and Oreston; Admiral's Hard to Cremyll (Mount Edgcumbe); and Mutton Cove to Cremyll.

CALSTOCK 1890 24549

These ships are topsail schooners and what might be an inside or outside Tamar barge at Calstock, 17 miles up-river from the sea. This small but busy inland port was heavily used by the local mining and quarrying industries. The inside barges, or Tamar sloops, carried cargoes between the various wharves and landing stages along the river; the outside barges, which were bigger and carried a topsail, were capable of undertaking coastal work between Plymouth and Falmouth and the Channel Islands.

FALMOUTH, THE HARBOUR 1895 37047

This photograph was possibly taken around the time of the regatta, though Falmouth was always a busy place. In the distance is an excursion paddler, though also in the picture are a Falmouth oyster catcher, a quay punt, and a number of transom-stern pilchard drivers. The smartly turned out crew of the boat pulling away from the quayside could be from a private yacht or even a warship.

FALMOUTH, THE MARKET STRAND 1890 24208

Like Greek waiters standing outside their tavernas, crewmen do their best to tempt tourists into parting with a shilling or two. As well as excursions up the Fal, ferries operated to Flushing and St Mawes Castle. Larger excursion steamers were employed on runs to the Lizard and Penzance. The boat on the far right might be the River Fal Steamship Co's 'New Resolute', built at Malpas, Cornwall in 1882. Of wood construction, she weighed 40 tons. She was later fitted with an enclosed wheelhouse.

PADSTOW
The Harbour 1901 47715

Most of the coastal trading vessels working out of Padstow were
schooners or ketches, and many earned their keep beach trading.
Though by 1901 the railways had captured a large percentage of
what had previously been sea-borne freight, there were areas where
it was still viable to move bulk, and even general cargo, by coaster.
Many of the vessels employed in the beach trade were old when
they came to it, costing their new owners between £200 and £500.
They would run onto a beach and wait for the tide to go out; then
the cargo would be loaded into horse-drawn carts, and the vessels
would float off on the incoming tide. The business was effectively
killed off around Cornwall after World War I; lorry ownership
rocketed as the military sold off surplus vehicles at give-away prices.

◆

FALMOUTH 1904 53033

By 1900, steamships well and truly dominated the world's merchant fleets, accounting for 72 per cent of world tonnage. Between 1900 and 1910 Britain's merchant fleet (not including the Dominion and colonial fleets) rose from 13.2 to 17.5 million tons. Over the same period the number of sailing ships in the fleet fell from 1.7 million to 750,000 tons. In 1905, freight rates for coal from the Welsh ports to the Plate varied between 6s 3d and 12s per ton. The rates for grain from Australia to the UK varied between 22s 6d and 26s 3d per ton.

NEWLYN, THE HARBOUR 1893 31797

This picture, which features the old quay, was taken some months before the completion of the new harbour. During the mackerel season, Newlyn bustled with freelance boatmen who earned their living ferrying the catch in clinker-built rowing boats known as bummers' gigs from fishing boats anchored offshore to waiting salesmen on the quayside. The practice died out during the early years of the 20th century with the introduction of steam drifters that were equipped to land catches directly on to the jetties.

MOUSEHOLE, THE HARBOUR 1893 31804

One mile south of Newlyn, Mousehole's medieval harbour drains completely at low water. One advantage its fishermen enjoy over many other villages along this part of the Cornish coast is that the harbour faces east, away from the prevailing south-westerly gales. There are few old buildings in the village, as it was almost completely destroyed by a Spanish raiding force in 1595. Still, they made a change from the French.

CHARLESTOWN, THE HARBOUR 1904 53050

The principal export from the tiny south Cornish port of Charlestown was china clay, much of it bound for Runcorn; from there it would be forwarded on to the Potteries. The principal import was Lancashire and North Staffordshire coal from Runcorn. A vessel arriving from Runcorn would discharge at a coal berth and then move over to a china clay berth to load. That was the theory, but the harbour could be so jammed up with ships that the move could involve several other vessels all being shunted around in a series of moves choreographed by the dock master.

NEWQUAY, THE HARBOUR 1894 33522
Newquay was developed in the 1830s for the export of china clay, copper and tin and the import of coal, fertiliser, timber and general cargo for the surrounding area. This photograph shows the local shipyard-built schooners and ketches.

SARK, CREUX HARBOUR 1894 33872
The Guernsey Steam Tug & Trading Co's 'Assistance' appears to have been on a luggage run, as cases and trunks are being unloaded and placed upon a cart. 'Assistance' undertook towing and general work around the Channel Islands.

ST IVES 1890 24178
The Frith archive contains a number of these posed group pictures; the majority seem to have been taken during the 1890s. The children are bare-footed, not just because they are on the beach; boots were worn only on Sundays. The exception is the young boy perched somewhat precariously upon the small boat; he appears to be wearing sea boots and a fishing smock.

ST IVES, LIFEBOATMEN 1906 56543
Members of the St Ives lifeboat wear the cork life-jacket designed in 1854 by Capt John Ross Ward. Cumbersome though it may look to us today, Ward's jacket worked. In 1861 the Whitby lifeboat, which was not a part of the RNLI establishment, was wrecked. The sole survivor was Henry Freeman, the only member of the crew with a Ward life-jacket.

ST IVES
The Harbour 1908 61074A

St Ives mackerel and pilchard drivers were of a similar design, the latter being the smaller version. Both were carvel-built. By the late 19th century the mackerel boat had developed into a two-masted fully decked craft up to 50ft in length. The pilchard drivers came in at around 30ft in length; until the 1890s they had been open-decked. During the autumn the pilchard boats also went after herring.

◆

POLPERRO, THE HARBOUR 1901 47794

The great gale of 1891 destroyed the bulk of the Polperro fishing fleet, and resulted in the harbour walls being extended to create a narrow entrance that could be closed off with timber baulks should the need arise. These post-gale craft have small cuddy decks forward. This late 19th-century improvement afforded the fishermen some protection from the weather. Prior to this, men slept in the bottom of the boats with nothing more than a canvas sheet or sail for protection against the elements.

PORTLEVEN, THE HARBOUR 1904 52276

Portleven was noted for building pilchard drivers and Bristol Channel pilot cutters. Local firms included John Bowden's yard, which was active between 1877 and 1905 -it can be seen in the background of this picture; Richard Kitto (later Kitto & Sons) was in business from 1864 to c1904.

PORTREATH
The Harbour 1898 41628

Portreath was little more than a fishing village until it was chosen
by Francis Basset (later Lord de Dunstanville) as an ideal
location from which to ship copper ore from the mines around
Redruth to Wales. In the background is the incline of the
Poldice-Portreath Tramroad. Constructed between 1809 and
1810, the tramway connected the mines at Gwennap and St Day
with the harbour. The incline was worked by a steam engine, and
motive power on the level sections was provided by horses and
mules. By the mid 19th century the harbour was handling
fourteen ships a week, taking copper out and bringing coal and
lime in. As with Polperro, the harbour entrance could be sealed
during bad weather with timber baulks.

MEVAGISSEY, THE HARBOUR c1884 16787

Five miles south of St Austell, Mevagissey is first recorded in 1410. The local class of pilchard driver and long liner was about 40ft in length with a beam of 12ft. Boats can still operate in and out of this harbour when weather conditions close those that face the prevailing south-westerlies.

MEVAGISSEY, THE HARBOUR 1904 52249

In 1740 Mevagissey ranked fourth among the Cornish pilchard ports, which between them had built up a lucrative trade exporting millions of pilchards each year to places like Italy. Around the end of the 19th and the beginning of the 20th century, the majority of large fishing boats at Mevagissey had originated from elsewhere in Cornwall, mainly from the west.

MEVAGISSEY 1898
The crew are sorting the catch. Many boats were half 'n halfers of 30ft to 40ft in length, and suitable for drift netting pilchards, herring or mackerel.

◆

FOWEY
The Harbour 1898
A three-masted barque and a brig lie at anchor below Hall Walk. Local ships traded to the Mediterranean, Spain and Portugal, and the last square-rigged merchant sailing ship on the British register was from Fowey. She was the 'Waterwitch', built at Poole in 1871 as a collier-brig, but converted to barquentine-rig in the 1880s. Owned by Edward Stephens, she made her last passage with cargo in 1936.

MEVAGISSEY 1898 41398A

FOWEY, THE HARBOUR 1898 41958

FOWEY, THE HARBOUR 1901 47696

FOWEY
The Harbour 1901

Fowey is crowded with all manner of craft, from rowing boats to private steam yachts. The ships anchored in the foreground are waiting to load with china clay. Their galley houses have been unbolted from their main decks and moved to one side in order for the ships to clear the clay tips.

LOOE
Fishermen 1906

This is one of Frith's posed groups. The fisherman on the right is well protected from the elements. His heavy seaboots would have been made of leather, and would have to have been greased regularly in order to keep them both supple and waterproof.

LOOE, FISHERMEN 1906 56415

LOOE 1893 32374

As a port, Looe declined with the coming of the railways, though it continued to maintain a fishing fleet; there were also exports of granite from local quarries, which was used for harbours, breakwaters and bridges. At the cutting edge of equal opportunities, even in the 19th century, the women of Looe, as well as looking after the children, cooking, washing and everything else, were expected to assist with loading and unloading cargo.

BUDE, THE CANAL 1893 31893

This is Bude Canal Sea Lock in 1893, two years after the waterway had been reduced to the 1.25 mile stretch to Rodd's Bridge; in reality it was little more than an extension of the harbour, which continued to handle cargo for the area. Note the lock gates, which are operated by manually worked crab winches.

BUDE
The Canal 1890 23782

Opened in 1823, the Bude Canal served a large area of north
Cornwall. The canal itself extended some 35 miles inland, though
by the time this picture was taken much of it had already closed. Its
most striking feature was its inclined planes; the nearest one to
Bude was at Marhamchurch, where the incline rose 120ft in 836ft.
The canal's tub-boats were fitted with wheels so that they could
travel up or down the inclines by means of cables; it was a method
that saved an absolute fortune on building locks, and represented a
practical solution to what otherwise would have been an
engineering and financial nightmare.

◆

BRISTOL DOCKS 1887 20133

No longer England's second port, Bristol was still busy handling imports for the west of England. By 1887 sail was far from finished; the new Bessemer steel-making process opened a window of opportunity for merchant sailing ship owners with the construction of large steel-hulled full-rigged ships. Fitted with labour-saving devices such as steam-powered windlasses and halyard winches, these big ships found employment in the bulk cargo trade; they carried nitrate, coal, grain, guano and timber. In 1887 the British merchant fleet carried 140 million tons of cargo, of which 49.3 million tons was coal; 12.1 million tons timber, and 19.2 million tons grain.

BRISTOL DOCKS 1900 45555

A screw tug prepares to assist a steamer to its berth in the Floating Harbour. Bristol developed to become a major centre for the importation of timber for use throughout the west of England. In 1870 it handled 105,000 tons, and by 1900 it was dealing with over 170,000 tons a year. During the same period, annual tobacco imports through the docks rose from 349 tons in 1880 to 2278 in 1910, and by the mid 1920s the average was 24,000 tons a year. As well as tugs, other service vessels included dredgers and lighters. Of the latter were the 'Garth', 'Maesteg', 'Rhymney' and 'Rhondda', between 156 and 170 gt and belonging to the Bristol Lighterage Co (a subsidiary of Elder Dempster). These small vessels undertook lighterage between Bristol and Avonmouth for Elders ships.

CARDIFF, THE DOCKS 1893 32696

Cardiff Docks were developed during the late 1830s by the 2nd Marquess of Bute, and were enlarged in the 1880s and again in the early 1900s. The opening of Roath Dock in 1887 gave Cardiff a further 33 acres of deep water shiphandling facilities. This was linked in 1907 to the newly-built Queen Alexandra Dock (52 acres) and the Roath Basin (1000ft x 550ft covering 13 acres) by a lock 600ft long x 80ft wide. Other facilities at Cardiff included the East Dock and Basin, covering 46 acres, and the West Dock and Basin, 200ft wide and with quayage totalling 4000ft.

BARRY DOCKS 1899 43450

Situated eight miles south-west of Cardiff, Barry was the last of the great Welsh coal ports to be developed. No 1 Dock, covering 73 acres of deep water, opened in 1889 and was equipped with nineteen coal hoists. No 2 Dock, covering 34 acres of deep water, opened in 1898; the north side for coal, the south side for general cargo, and the eastern end for timber, with timber ponds covering 34 acres and six acres respectively. No 3 Dock, or the Basin, was the tidal entrance, but could accommodate some general cargo. The ship nearest the camera is Turnbull, Scott & Co's 'Eastgate', which was built in their family-owned shipyard at of Thomas Turnbull & Son, Whitby. The yard was opened in 1840 to build wooden ships, but in 1871 production was switched to building iron tramps. A total of 113 were built between then and the yard's closure in 1902. Of these, sixty were built for the Turnbull family themselves for their fleets at Whitby, Cardiff and London. The reason for the yard's closure was that Whitby bridge restricted dimensions to a maximum beam of 44ft.

BARRY DOCKS 1899 43451A

In the late 1890s, one last stronghold of the big iron and steel square-rigged ships was in the bulk cargo trade, where they could compete on operating costs and freight rates with steamships. But here too they were under threat. In 1897, London hiked the insurance rates for sail tonnage, especially on older vessels engaged in the wool trade, forcing companies such as the Aberdeen Line to sell off some of their ships. A further blow came on 5 June 1899 with the collapse of the Anglo-Boer conference, called to settle by negotiation the problems of the Transvaal. With war inevitable, the British Government immediately began to requisition steamships; these included twenty British India Steam Navigation vessels, who were ordered to land their passengers without delay and embark troops. The ensuing Boer War led to a recovery in freight rates for steam tonnage. Many ships were taken on permanent charter to transport men, animals, equipment and stores to the conflict.

BARRY DOCKS 1899 43451B
The South Shields-built steamer 'Margaret Jones' has taken on coal, and prepares to clear Barry. Coal played a major role in British shipping for decades; it was exported not only to customers in other countries, but to maintain stocks world-wide at the coaling stations of the Royal Navy and bunkering ports alike. The Naval Estimates for 1892-93 budgeted £532,000 for coal for use in steam vessels and a further £63,000 for coal used in dockyards.

SWANSEA, SOUTH DOCK 1906 54952
With the opening in 1920 of the Queen's Dock, Swansea Docks covered an area of 269 acres. South Dock opened in 1859, followed by the Prince of Wales Dock in 1891 (extended in 1898) and the King's Dock in 1904.

PORTMADOC
The Harbour 1908 60718

Portmadoc handled slate traffic from both south Caernarvon and
north Merioneth; the schooners were able to call upon the services
of a tug for towing either in or out of the harbour. If the date of
the picture is correct, 1908 is quite late for a paddle-tug to be
serving at other than a major coal port such as Cardiff, Sunderland
or Seaham. Though paddle-tugs were built for manoeuvrability,
they lacked the power of screw tugs, and they were becoming
expensive to operate as coal and labour costs increased. The
Portmadoc based paddle-tug 'Snowdon', built in 1885, was sold off
in 1900 to John Dry, South Shields. She served with various north-
east tug companies until she was finally withdrawn in 1949.

PORTMADOC, THE HARBOUR 1908 60721

Portmadoc was originally intended to be the port of Tremadoc, a new town that never got beyond a village; it was planned by the speculator William Madocks, who had a grand scheme to persuade the Government to ditch Holyhead as the principal port for mails to Ireland. However, thanks to the slate industry, Portmadoc developed on its own. In 1836, a narrow gauge railway nine miles long opened to connect the quarries at Blaenau Ffestiniog with Portmadoc harbour. Here slate schooners line the wharves, and slates awaiting shipment are stacked in their thousands.

CAERNARVON 1891 29499

Schooners lie alongside the slate quay at Caernarvon. It was from here and Bangor that slate from the Snowdon area was shipped to various European ports. From the 1870s many owners invested in three-masted schooners that not only displaced brigs and even brigantines on the coastal trade, but were ideal for the salt fish trade from Newfoundland.

Working Boats

FRASERBURGH c1900 F63002

The zulu is considered to have been one of the finest fore- and mizzen-
rigged lugger designs of the late 19th century. The craft was a hybrid,
incorporating features of the scaffie and fifie, and ranging in size from 60ft
to 80ft in length, though a number of 120-footers were eventually built.
Zulus carried a large amount of canvas, and the bigger boats had holds
capable of taking 70 to 80 tons of herring. The subject of our picture
mounts a double flywheel hand capstan.

FRASERBURGH C1900 F63003

There are several stories as to how the zulu got its name, but the first of the type does appear to have been built around 1879 at the time of the Zulu War. It was as a direct result of changing to carvel building that the overall length of zulus increased. The masts had no standing rigging, being supported by the sail halyard and burton stay tackle. Note the mast on PF114: at deck level it appears to be at least two feet thick. The zulu beam to length ratio was in the order of 1:4. In later variants the tiller was replaced by steering wheels; steam capstans, which were used to work both rigging and the trawl, came as standard.

NEWHAVEN 1897 39139

Fifies came in all sizes. There were fully decked seventy-footers, built with oak keels, frames and Norwegian pine masts, which were used to chase herring in the summer and for lining in the autumn. Then there were the much smaller double-ended open boats known as fifie yawls, which were employed for haddock lining in winter and spring.

SCARBOROUGH 1890 23465

Here we see boats from a variety of ports, including Hull and Penzance. SH412 is a Scarborough yawl, a type primarily employed on lining or drift net fishing for herring, though some were converted for trawling. Yawls varied in length from about 45ft to 60ft, were ketch-rigged and sported elegant lute sterns. The ability to remain at sea for several days meant that the yawls could exploit less crowded areas of the North Sea beyond the busy herring grounds.

SCARBOROUGH 1890 23467

The crews of several Lowestoft-registered trawlers take advantage of low water to carry out maintenance on the hulls of their vessels. Note that the capstan fires are kept lit. This seems to have quickly developed into a tradition with Lowestoft skippers so that they could set sail immediately upon leaving a port. It was standard practice on these boats to run the sheets and halyards through the steam capstan, enabling the capstan operator (usually the skipper) to handle the sails by himself.

BRIDLINGTON, THE QUAY 1893 32050

Square-sterned cobles carrying a single lug sail, but capable of deploying a jib upon their long bowsprits, earn their keep taking trippers on excursions round the bay. Cobles came in all lengths from 10ft to 40ft, and usually carried a single large lug sail, but the rig could, and did, vary.

SHERINGHAM 1893 33313

The crew of a Sheringham crab boat pose for the camera. These clinker built, double-ended open boats were approximately 18ft long and carried a dipping lug sail of up to 120 sq ft. The hull was shaped to allow the boat to ride through the breakers to the shore; the crew then used the oars protruding from orruck holes to carry the boat up the beach. The origins of these craft are obscure, though some their features could suggest a Danish influence.

SURBITON 1896 38336

This photograph shows two spirit-rigged Thames river barges at Messenger's Boat House, Surbiton. The heavily-laden 'Glasgow' will come alongside to discharge her cargo once the other barge has finished unloading a cargo of what looks like coke.

BROADSTAIRS
The Harbour 1897 39592
There were several variants of the Thames sailing barge. Whilst
some were capable of undertaking coastal but not deep sea trade,
others were confined to the Thames and its navigable tributaries.
The coastal barges were over 80ft in length, with a beam of 19ft
and draught when laden of between six and seven feet. They could
carry between 120 and 150 tons of cargo, and were crewed by a
skipper and two men. These spiritsail barges carried over 2000
square feet of canvas; the small mizzen sail was sheeted to the
rudder to assist tiller steering. In the late 1890s there were over
2000 Thames barges in service.

PLYMOUTH, THE BARBICAN 1890 22474

Plymouth hookers were essentially long liners, varying in size from 25ft to 40ft and from between five and fourteen tons. During the 1880s and 1890s there were about 200 hookers registered locally, and as they rarely spent more than twenty-four hours at sea, much of the town's fresh fish was landed from them. By the time this picture was taken, a few were working with light trawling gear.

MULLION 1890 24255

During the late 19th century, crabbers could be found working out of many a Cornish cove. They were small open boats of either carvel or clinker build, usually between 16ft and 20ft in length; but as with most things nautical, there were always exceptions, all with a good carrying capacity. Note the communal capstan for hauling boats up above the tide line.

POLPERRO 1888 21270
Fewer than six miles from Fowey, Polperro is first recorded as being a fishing village in 1303. This picture was taken before the construction of the counter pier; this was built so that the entrance to the harbour could be closed off with timber baulks during bad weather. The boat is a Polperro sprittie.

MEVAGISSEY, THE HARBOUR 1904 52248
Toshers, crabbers, pilchard and mackerel drivers fill Mevagissey Harbour. The tosher, an example of which is the small white open-hulled sailing craft in the foreground, was a local class of hand liner. As can be seen here, the hull was divided into compartments, and though this example is open-decked throughout, larger toshers were often fitted with a small cuddy deck forward.

PENZANCE 1890 22978

There were over 100 first class luggers registered at Penzance in the early 1890s. Fully decked, and ranging in length from about 45ft to 55ft and from 14 to 25 tons, these boats were employed chasing mackerel. Note that the foremast stands vertical, whilst the mizzen has a distinctive forward rake. On these craft the mizzen was taller than the foremast.

CLOVELLY, THE HARBOUR 1890 24770

Clovelly long boomers have their trawls hauled aloft to dry. These carvel-built, decked smacks could be seen fishing the upper reaches of the Bristol Channel. They were called long boomers simply because of the length of the boom overhanging the stern. The small two-masted luggers with the heart-shaped transoms are Clovelly picarooners; this name is said to be derived from the Spanish for searobber. Picarooners were about 13ft long, and were employed in the herring fishery.

PORT ST MARY 1901 47236

This photograph shows a de-rigged Manx nobby at Port St Mary. Nobbies and
nickies had the same basic hull shape, but were rigged differently, and the nickey
was probably the better sailor of the two. During the second half of the 19th century
it became common practice for boats to go into south-east Irish waters and fish for
mackerel from March to June, to return to Man for the herring season, and then
from October to follow the herring into Scottish waters. The fleet was at its height
in the early 1870s with over 400 craft of varying types on the register. But the 1880s
and 1890s brought with them a period of decline. In 1881 the Peel herring fleet
consisted of 309 boats employing 2163 men and boys; the annual catch was worth
around £11,000. By 1891 the local fleet was down to 174 boats employing 860 men
and boys and landing an annual catch valued at just under £3000. By the mid 1890s,
the Port St Mary fleet had shrunk to just 56 boats employing 346 men and boys; it
too was landing a catch worth less than £3000 a year.

Index

Aberdour 33

Aldeburgh 84

Barry Docks 115, 116, 117

Belfast 46, 47 48

Bideford 94

Boston 78, 79

Bridlington 124

Brighton 37

Bristol 113, 114

Brixham 95

Broadstairs 126

Bude 111, 112

Caernarvon 119

Calstock 96

Cardiff 114

Charlestown 100

Clovelly 129

Devonport 18, 23, 24, 96

Douglas 67, 68, 69

Dover 28–29

Dublin 49, 50–51

Dunoon 32

Exeter 91, 92

Falmouth 97, 99

Fleetwood 44, 45, 46, 66

Folkestone 85

Fort Perch Rock 54

Fowey 109, 110

Fraserburgh 120, 121

Gravesend 22, 37

Great Yarmouth 80

Greenock 34–35

Grimsby 77, 78

Hartlepool 74

Helensburgh 72

Hull 74, 75, 76

Kings Lyn 79

Kingstown 20, 21

Liverpool 19, 20, 55, 56, 57, 58, 60–61

Llandudno 36

London 82–83

Looe 110, 111

Lowestoft 81

Lulworth Cove 40

Lyme Regis 90

Manchester 62–63, 64

Mevagissey 108, 109, 128

Mousehole 100

Mullion 127

Newhaven 73, 121

Newlyn 99

Newquay 101

Padstow 98

Penzance 129

Perch Rock Lighthouse 52–53

Plymouth 25, 127

Polperro 106, 128

Poole 41

Port St Mary 130

Portleven 106

Portmadoc 118, 119

Portreath 107

Portsmouth Harbour 26–27, 28, 29

Preston Docks 65

Ramsgate 86–87

Rochester 84

Rothesay 30–31, 70–71

Runcorn 59

Rye 88

St Helier 42–43

St Ives 102–103, 104, 105

Salcombe 93

Sark 101

Scarborough 122–123, 124

Sheringham 125

Southampton 89

Surbiton 125

Swansea 117

West Bay 91

Weymouth 38, 39

Frith Book Co Titles

www.francisfrith.co.uk

The Frith Book Company publishes over 100 new titles each year. A selection of those currently available are listed below. For latest catalogue please contact Frith Book Co.

Town Books 96 pages, approx 100 photos. County and Themed Books 128 pages, approx 150 photos (unless specified). All titles hardback laminated case and jacket except those indicated pb (paperback)

Amersham, Chesham & Rickmansworth (pb)			Derby (pb)	1-85937-367-4	£9.99
	1-85937-340-2	£9.99	Derbyshire (pb)	1-85937-196-5	£9.99
Ancient Monuments & Stone Circles	1-85937-143-4	£17.99	Devon (pb)	1-85937-297-x	£9.99
Aylesbury (pb)	1-85937-227-9	£9.99	Dorset (pb)	1-85937-269-4	£9.99
Bakewell	1-85937-113-2	£12.99	Dorset Churches	1-85937-172-8	£17.99
Barnstaple (pb)	1-85937-300-3	£9.99	Dorset Coast (pb)	1-85937-299-6	£9.99
Bath (pb)	1-85937419-0	£9.99	Dorset Living Memories	1-85937-210-4	£14.99
Bedford (pb)	1-85937-205-8	£9.99	Down the Severn	1-85937-118-3	£14.99
Berkshire (pb)	1-85937-191-4	£9.99	Down the Thames (pb)	1-85937-278-3	£9.99
Berkshire Churches	1-85937-170-1	£17.99	Down the Trent	1-85937-311-9	£14.99
Blackpool (pb)	1-85937-382-8	£9.99	Dublin (pb)	1-85937-231-7	£9.99
Bognor Regis (pb)	1-85937-431-x	£9.99	East Anglia (pb)	1-85937-265-1	£9.99
Bournemouth	1-85937-067-5	£12.99	East London	1-85937-080-2	£14.99
Bradford (pb)	1-85937-204-x	£9.99	East Sussex	1-85937-130-2	£14.99
Brighton & Hove(pb)	1-85937-192-2	£8.99	Eastbourne	1-85937-061-6	£12.99
Bristol (pb)	1-85937-264-3	£9.99	Edinburgh (pb)	1-85937-193-0	£8.99
British Life A Century Ago (pb)	1-85937-213-9	£9.99	England in the 1880s	1-85937-331-3	£17.99
Buckinghamshire (pb)	1-85937-200-7	£9.99	English Castles (pb)	1-85937-434-4	£9.99
Camberley (pb)	1-85937-222-8	£9.99	English Country Houses	1-85937-161-2	£17.99
Cambridge (pb)	1-85937-422-0	£9.99	Essex (pb)	1-85937-270-8	£9.99
Cambridgeshire (pb)	1-85937-420-4	£9.99	Exeter	1-85937-126-4	£12.99
Canals & Waterways (pb)	1-85937-291-0	£9.99	Exmoor	1-85937-132-9	£14.99
Canterbury Cathedral (pb)	1-85937-179-5	£9.99	Falmouth	1-85937-066-7	£12.99
Cardiff (pb)	1-85937-093-4	£9.99	Folkestone (pb)	1-85937-124-8	£9.99
Carmarthenshire	1-85937-216-3	£14.99	Glasgow (pb)	1-85937-190-6	£9.99
Chelmsford (pb)	1-85937-310-0	£9.99	Gloucestershire	1-85937-102-7	£14.99
Cheltenham (pb)	1-85937-095-0	£9.99	Great Yarmouth (pb)	1-85937-426-3	£9.99
Cheshire (pb)	1-85937-271-6	£9.99	Greater Manchester (pb)	1-85937-266-x	£9.99
Chester	1-85937-090-x	£12.99	Guildford (pb)	1-85937-410-7	£9.99
Chesterfield	1-85937-378-x	£9.99	Hampshire (pb)	1-85937-279-1	£9.99
Chichester (pb)	1-85937-228-7	£9.99	Hampshire Churches (pb)	1-85937-207-4	£9.99
Colchester (pb)	1-85937-188-4	£8.99	Harrogate	1-85937-423-9	£9.99
Cornish Coast	1-85937-163-9	£14.99	Hastings & Bexhill (pb)	1-85937-131-0	£9.99
Cornwall (pb)	1-85937-229-5	£9.99	Heart of Lancashire (pb)	1-85937-197-3	£9.99
Cornwall Living Memories	1-85937-248-1	£14.99	Helston (pb)	1-85937-214-7	£9.99
Cotswolds (pb)	1-85937-230-9	£9.99	Hereford (pb)	1-85937-175-2	£9.99
Cotswolds Living Memories	1-85937-255-4	£14.99	Herefordshire	1-85937-174-4	£14.99
County Durham	1-85937-123-x	£14.99	Hertfordshire (pb)	1-85937-247-3	£9.99
Croydon Living Memories	1-85937-162-0	£9.99	Horsham (pb)	1-85937-432-8	£9.99
Cumbria	1-85937-101-9	£14.99	Humberside	1-85937-215-5	£14.99
Dartmoor	1-85937-145-0	£14.99	Hythe, Romney Marsh & Ashford	1-85937-256-2	£9.99

Available from your local bookshop or from the publisher

Frith Book Co Titles (continued)

Title	ISBN	Price	Title	ISBN	Price
Ipswich (pb)	1-85937-424-7	£9.99	St Ives (pb)	1-85937415-8	£9.99
Ireland (pb)	1-85937-181-7	£9.99	Scotland (pb)	1-85937-182-5	£9.99
Isle of Man (pb)	1-85937-268-6	£9.99	Scottish Castles (pb)	1-85937-323-2	£9.99
Isles of Scilly	1-85937-136-1	£14.99	Sevenoaks & Tunbridge	1-85937-057-8	£12.99
Isle of Wight (pb)	1-85937-429-8	£9.99	Sheffield, South Yorks (pb)	1-85937-267-8	£9.99
Isle of Wight Living Memories	1-85937-304-6	£14.99	Shrewsbury (pb)	1-85937-325-9	£9.99
Kent (pb)	1-85937-189-2	£9.99	Shropshire (pb)	1-85937-326-7	£9.99
Kent Living Memories	1-85937-125-6	£14.99	Somerset	1-85937-153-1	£14.99
Lake District (pb)	1-85937-275-9	£9.99	South Devon Coast	1-85937-107-8	£14.99
Lancaster, Morecambe & Heysham (pb)	1-85937-233-3	£9.99	South Devon Living Memories	1-85937-168-x	£14.99
Leeds (pb)	1-85937-202-3	£9.99	South Hams	1-85937-220-1	£14.99
Leicester	1-85937-073-x	£12.99	Southampton (pb)	1-85937-427-1	£9.99
Leicestershire (pb)	1-85937-185-x	£9.99	Southport (pb)	1-85937-425-5	£9.99
Lincolnshire (pb)	1-85937-433-6	£9.99	Staffordshire	1-85937-047-0	£12.99
Liverpool & Merseyside (pb)	1-85937-234-1	£9.99	Stratford upon Avon	1-85937-098-5	£12.99
London (pb)	1-85937-183-3	£9.99	Suffolk (pb)	1-85937-221-x	£9.99
Ludlow (pb)	1-85937-176-0	£9.99	Suffolk Coast	1-85937-259-7	£14.99
Luton (pb)	1-85937-235-x	£9.99	Surrey (pb)	1-85937-240-6	£9.99
Maidstone	1-85937-056-x	£14.99	Sussex (pb)	1-85937-184-1	£9.99
Manchester (pb)	1-85937-198-1	£9.99	Swansea (pb)	1-85937-167-1	£9.99
Middlesex	1-85937-158-2	£14.99	Tees Valley & Cleveland	1-85937-211-2	£14.99
New Forest	1-85937-128-0	£14.99	Thanet (pb)	1-85937-116-7	£9.99
Newark (pb)	1-85937-366-6	£9.99	Tiverton (pb)	1-85937-178-7	£9.99
Newport, Wales (pb)	1-85937-258-9	£9.99	Torbay	1-85937-063-2	£12.99
Newquay (pb)	1-85937-421-2	£9.99	Truro	1-85937-147-7	£12.99
Norfolk (pb)	1-85937-195-7	£9.99	Victorian and Edwardian Cornwall	1-85937-252-x	£14.99
Norfolk Living Memories	1-85937-217-1	£14.99	Victorian & Edwardian Devon	1-85937-253-8	£14.99
Northamptonshire	1-85937-150-7	£14.99	Victorian & Edwardian Kent	1-85937-149-3	£14.99
Northumberland Tyne & Wear (pb)	1-85937-281-3	£9.99	Vic & Ed Maritime Album	1-85937-144-2	£17.99
North Devon Coast	1-85937-146-9	£14.99	Victorian and Edwardian Sussex	1-85937-157-4	£14.99
North Devon Living Memories	1-85937-261-9	£14.99	Victorian & Edwardian Yorkshire	1-85937-154-x	£14.99
North London	1-85937-206-6	£14.99	Victorian Seaside	1-85937-159-0	£17.99
North Wales (pb)	1-85937-298-8	£9.99	Villages of Devon (pb)	1-85937-293-7	£9.99
North Yorkshire (pb)	1-85937-236-8	£9.99	Villages of Kent (pb)	1-85937-294-5	£9.99
Norwich (pb)	1-85937-194-9	£8.99	Villages of Sussex (pb)	1-85937-295-3	£9.99
Nottingham (pb)	1-85937-324-0	£9.99	Warwickshire (pb)	1-85937-203-1	£9.99
Nottinghamshire (pb)	1-85937-187-6	£9.99	Welsh Castles (pb)	1-85937-322-4	£9.99
Oxford (pb)	1-85937-411-5	£9.99	West Midlands (pb)	1-85937-289-9	£9.99
Oxfordshire (pb)	1-85937-430-1	£9.99	West Sussex	1-85937-148-5	£14.99
Peak District (pb)	1-85937-280-5	£9.99	West Yorkshire (pb)	1-85937-201-5	£9.99
Penzance	1-85937-069-1	£12.99	Weymouth (pb)	1-85937-209-0	£9.99
Peterborough (pb)	1-85937-219-8	£9.99	Wiltshire (pb)	1-85937-277-5	£9.99
Piers	1-85937-237-6	£17.99	Wiltshire Churches (pb)	1-85937-171-x	£9.99
Plymouth	1-85937-119-1	£12.99	Wiltshire Living Memories	1-85937-245-7	£14.99
Poole & Sandbanks (pb)	1-85937-251-1	£9.99	Winchester (pb)	1-85937-428-x	£9.99
Preston (pb)	1-85937-212-0	£9.99	Windmills & Watermills	1-85937-242-2	£17.99
Reading (pb)	1-85937-238-4	£9.99	Worcester (pb)	1-85937-165-5	£9.99
Romford (pb)	1-85937-319-4	£9.99	Worcestershire	1-85937-152-3	£14.99
Salisbury (pb)	1-85937-239-2	£9.99	York (pb)	1-85937-199-x	£9.99
Scarborough (pb)	1-85937-379-8	£9.99	Yorkshire (pb)	1-85937-186-8	£9.99
St Albans (pb)	1-85937-341-0	£9.99	Yorkshire Living Memories	1-85937-166-3	£14.99

See Frith books on the internet www.francisfrith.co.uk

FRITH PRODUCTS & SERVICES

Francis Frith would doubtless be pleased to know that the pioneering publishing venture he started in 1860 still continues today. A hundred and forty years later, The Francis Frith Collection continues in the same innovative tradition and is now one of the foremost publishers of vintage photographs in the world. Some of the current activities include:

Interior Decoration

Today Frith's photographs can be seen framed and as giant wall murals in thousands of pubs, restaurants, hotels, banks, retail stores and other public buildings throughout the country. In every case they enhance the unique local atmosphere of the places they depict and provide reminders of gentler days in an increasingly busy and frenetic world.

Product Promotions

Frith products are used by many major companies to promote the sales of their own products or to reinforce their own history and heritage. Frith promotions have been used by Hovis bread, Courage beers, Scots Porage Oats, Colman's mustard, Cadbury's foods, Mellow Birds coffee, Dunhill pipe tobacco, Guinness, and Bulmer's Cider.

Genealogy and Family History

As the interest in family history and roots grows world-wide, more and more people are turning to Frith's photographs of Great Britain for images of the towns, villages and streets where their ancestors lived; and, of course, photographs of the churches and chapels where their ancestors were christened, married and buried are an essential part of every genealogy tree and family album.

Frith Products

All Frith photographs are available Framed or just as Mounted Prints and Posters (size 23 x 16 inches). These may be ordered from the address below. From time to time other products - Address Books, Calendars, Table Mats, etc - are available.

The Internet

Already twenty thousand Frith photographs can be viewed and purchased on the internet through the Frith websites and a myriad of partner sites.

For more detailed information on Frith companies and products, look at these sites:

www.francisfrith.co.uk
www.francisfrith.com
(for North American visitors)

See the complete list of Frith Books at:
www.francisfrith.co.uk
This web site is regularly updated with the latest list of publications from the Frith Book Company. If you wish to buy books relating to another part of the country that your local bookshop does not stock, you may purchase on-line.

For further information, trade, or author enquiries please contact us at the address below:
The Francis Frith Collection, Frith's Barn, Teffont, Salisbury, Wiltshire, England SP3 5QP.
Tel: +44 (0)1722 716 376 Fax: +44 (0)1722 716 881 Email: sales@francisfrith.co.uk

See Frith books on the internet www.francisfrith.co.uk

TO RECEIVE YOUR FREE MOUNTED PRINT

Mounted Print
Overall size 14 x 11 inches

Cut out this Voucher and return it with your remittance for £1.95 to cover postage and handling, to UK addresses. For overseas addresses please include £4.00 post and handling. Choose any photograph included in this book. Your SEPIA print will be A4 in size, and mounted in a cream mount with burgundy rule line, overall size 14 x 11 inches.

Order additional Mounted Prints at HALF PRICE (only £7.49 each*)

If there are further pictures you would like to order, possibly as gifts for friends and family, purchase them at half price (no additional postage and handling required).

Have your Mounted Prints framed*

For an additional £14.95 per print you can have your chosen Mounted Print framed in an elegant polished wood and gilt moulding, overall size 16 x 13 inches (no additional postage and handling required).

---

* IMPORTANT!
These special prices are only available if ordered using the original voucher on this page (no copies permitted) and at the same time as your free Mounted Print, for delivery to the same address

---

Frith Collectors' Guild

From time to time we publish a magazine of news and stories about Frith photographs and further special offers of Frith products. If you would like 12 months FREE membership, please return this form.

Send completed forms to:
The Francis Frith Collection, Frith's Barn, Teffont, Salisbury, Wiltshire SP3 5QP

Voucher for FREE and Reduced Price Frith Prints

Picture no.	Page number	Qty	Mounted @ £7.49	Framed + £14.95	Total Cost
		1	**Free of charge***	£	£
			£7.49	£	£
			£7.49	£	£
			£7.49	£	£
			£7.49	£	£
			£7.49	£	£

Please allow 28 days for delivery	*** Post & handling**	**£1.95**
Book Title	**Total Order Cost**	**£**

Please do not photocopy this voucher. Only the original is valid, so please cut it out and return it to us.

I enclose a cheque / postal order for £ . . . .
made payable to 'The Francis Frith Collection'
OR please debit my Mastercard / Visa / Switch / Amex card
(credit cards please on all overseas orders)

Number . . . .

Issue No(Switch only) . . . . .Valid from (Amex/Switch) . . . .

Expires . . . . Signature . . . .

Name Mr/Mrs/Ms . . . .

Address . . . .

. . . .

. . . . Postcode . . . .

Daytime Tel No . . . .   Valid to 31/12/03

The Francis Frith Collectors' Guild

Please enrol me as a member for 12 months free of charge.

Name Mr/Mrs/Ms . . . .

Address . . . .

. . . .

. . . . Postcode . . . .

Would you like to find out more about Francis Frith?

We have recently recruited some entertaining speakers who are happy to visit local groups, clubs and societies to give an illustrated talk documenting Frith's travels and photographs. If you are a member of such a group and are interested in hosting a presentation, we would love to hear from you.

Our speakers bring with them a small selection of our local town and county books, together with sample prints. They are happy to take orders. A small proportion of the order value is donated to the group who have hosted the presentation. The talks are therefore an excellent way of fundraising for small groups and societies.

Can you help us with information about any of the Frith photographs in this book?

We are gradually compiling an historical record for each of the photographs in the Frith archive. It is always fascinating to find out the names of the people shown in the pictures, as well as insights into the shops, buildings and other features depicted.

If you recognize anyone in the photographs in this book, or if you have information not already included in the author's caption, do let us know. We would love to hear from you, and will try to publish it in future books or articles.

Our production team

Frith books are produced by a small dedicated team at offices in the converted Grade II listed 18th-century barn at Teffont near Salisbury, illustrated above. Most have worked with the Frith Collection for many years. All have in common one quality: they have a passion for the Frith Collection. The team is constantly expanding, but currently includes:

Jason Buck, John Buck, Douglas Burns, Heather Crisp, Lucy Elcock, Isobel Hall, Rob Hames, Hazel Heaton, Peter Horne, James Kinnear, Tina Leary, Hannah Marsh, Eliza Sackett, Terence Sackett, Sandra Sanger, Lewis Taylor, Shelley Tolcher, Helen Vimpany, Clive Wathen and Jenny Wathen.

Free Print – see overleaf